The Tate Gallery

an illustrated companion to the National Collections of British & Modern Foreign Art

THE TATE GALLERY

ISBN 0 905005 46 5 (paperbound)
ISBN 0 905005 47 3 (clothbound)
Published by order of the Trustees 1979.
Reprinted 1980; second edition 1981
Copyright © 1979 The Tate Gallery, London
Published by the Tate Gallery Publications Department,
Millbank, London SW1P 4RG
Designed by Sue Fowler
Printed in Great Britain by Balding & Mansell, Wisbech, Cambs.

Foreword

The first edition of this book was published to celebrate the opening in 1979 of the Tate Gallery's extension. It drew particular attention to the many fine works which had been acquired under my predecessors, Sir John Rothenstein and Sir Norman Reid.

Thanks to the generosity of our friends, benefactors, and of successive governments who provide our purchasing funds, the collection continues to grow. We are indeed fortunate to be able to go on building up fully representative and comprehensive collections of both Twentieth-century Art and British Painting of all periods. Some of the most recent acquisitions are mentioned in the pages that follow; others are too new to be included.

We are grateful to our regular visitors for their support, and hope that newcomers will return. Well over a million visitors each year make the not easy journey to visit the Tate, and our attendance figures are steadily growing.

A word of warning: all the works illustrated and discussed here may not at the moment be on exhibition in the galleries. Many loans are made from the collection and, in return of course, we are able to hold special exhibitions. These take up space, and despite the much increased gallery area that the 1979 extension provided, we are still unable to show as much as we would like. Most of the important paintings in the British Collection are on view, but in the Modern Collection we can show only a part of our holdings. Key works are almost always on exhibition in the main sequence of galleries, but other sections of the collection are shown on a rotating basis. The information desk will be happy to answer any queries you may have.

Fortunately we have now begun to build the Clore Gallery for the Turner Museum on the hospital site, adjacent to the Tate on the Westminster side. This is, we hope, only the first of a group of new buildings, designed by James Stirling. We would like eventually to add a Library and Archive building, a Museum of Art Now, and a Museum of Twentieth-century Art, so that the existing Tate Gallery building would become a Museum of British Art, with a collection continuing to the present day.

We must plan for the future, however difficult it may be to achieve such plans. A museum collecting modern art is alive, vigorous, and growing all the time. Enormous progress has been made at the Tate Gallery in the last thirty years, and I am confident that the next twenty will show equally dramatic achievements.

Alan Bowness, Director

The Tate Gallery

Millbank, London SW1P 4RG Telephone 01-828 1212

Times of opening

Gallery Monday–Saturday 10–6; Sunday 2–6
Restaurant Monday–Saturday 12–3; closed Sunday
Coffee Shop Monday–Saturday 10.30–5.30; Sunday 2–5.30
Gallery Shop Monday–Saturday 10–5.30; Sunday 2–5.30

Tate Gallery Publications

Turner at the Tate
92 paintings by J.M.W. Turner in the Tate Gallery collection,
reproduced in full-page colour, introduced by an essay on
'Turner and Colour' by Martin Butlin.
$8\frac{1}{4} \times 11\frac{3}{4}$ in. 112 pages, 92 illustrations. £4.95 paperbound

Catalogue of the Tate Gallery's Collection of Modern Art
other than works by British artists.
Compiled by Ronald Alley
$9\frac{1}{4} \times 7\frac{1}{2}$ in. 800 pages, 1,012 illustrations. £45 clothbound

The Tate Gallery Collections
Complete list of works in the Tate Gallery (and those by the same
artists in the National Gallery).
8×6 in, approx. 373 pages, £3.25

Complete Catalogue of Colour Prints
All the Tate Gallery reproductions available shown in full colour.
$8\frac{1}{4} \times 4\frac{1}{4}$ in, 72 pages, 140 illustrations, 50p

Catalogues of publications (books, posters, colour prints and
postcards), colour slides and greetings cards available from:

Tate Gallery Publications Department, Millbank, London SW1P 4RG
Telephone 01-834 5651

Contents

Cover
Front: George Stubbs, **Reapers** 1785 (detail)
Back: Henri Matisse, **The Snail** 1953

Painting in the Sixteenth and Seventeenth Centuries

John Bettes, **A Man in a Black Cap** 1545

The kind of painting invented by the Renaissance reached Britain late and developed fitfully. The greatest Renaissance artist to work in Britain was Holbein, who brought an unrivalled skill of eye and hand to the court of Henry VIII. The earliest picture in the Tate, the 'Man in a Black Cap' by John Bettes, was painted in 1545, two years after Holbein's death of the plague. Bettes' style was modelled on his, but by comparison with Holbein's cold and wiry power the portrayal is mild and respectful. Hans Eworth, who arrived from Antwerp at about the time the Bettes picture was painted, produced what might be termed a Flemish distillation of Holbein's manner, particularly in his delicate small-scale portraits such as the 'Lady Golding' of 1563, but gradually he moved towards painting more formal costume pieces dominated by flat, jewelled patterns. This shadowless style, approved by Queen Elizabeth as the best vehicle for presenting an image of heiratic and ageless dignity, sustained a poetry and concentrated passion of its own in the miniatures of her court painter Nicholas Hilliard, but these qualities tend to evaporate in the larger works painted in his manner. The portraits of Sir Thomas and Lady Kitson, painted in 1573 by Hilliard's contemporary George Gower, show a robust individual hand working in a style very distinct from that of Eworth. Paintings like these, however, show that although the representation of reality was competently understood by native painters, British taste preferred the intellectual organisation of a painting to remain at a heraldic level. As a result, a blunt realism came to be combined with archaic artifice in British painting in a manner unparalleled elsewhere. It produced the extraordinarily decorative costume pieces of the late sixteenth century, whose rigid stance is often softened by an intangible mood conveyed by masque dress or poetic inscriptions. They were supplied by a number of closely allied workshops, mostly of Flemish extraction, like those of the de Critz and Gheeraerts families. The richly austere portrait of Lady Harington of 1592, reasonably attributed to Marcus Gheeraerts the younger, is a splendid example of its kind, while the bright, flat shapes of 'The Cholmondeley Sisters' show that the same concern with fact and pattern appertained even at this level of anonymous journeyman's work.

The poetic patterning of the Elizabethan age was carried well into the seventeenth century, as can be seen in Robert Peake's portraits of two ladies of the Pope family, one of which is dated 1615, but the style was now old-fashioned. New painters from abroad like Paul Van Somer (another Fleming) brought to Britain some of the facility of Rubens and the sense of solid reality that was the common substance of Northern painting: his 'Elizabeth Grey, Countess of Kent' exists in a world of real air and solid flesh. Daniel Mytens brought from Holland the measured dignity and physical assurance displayed in 'The Duke of Hamilton as a Boy', while the complex allegories of the as yet unattributed 'William Style' could be by another Netherlandish artist responding as late as 1636 to an English love of fact and mood expressed through symbols that looks back to the Elizabethans.

British School, **The Cholmondeley Sisters** *c.*1600–10

Sir Anthony Van Dyck,
A Lady of the Spencer Family *c.*1633–8

Cornelius Johnson was born in London but was probably Dutch-trained. He modelled himself closely on Mytens and later Van Dyck, but the two little portrait heads of 1629 have a sweet-tempered attractiveness that was peculiar to him, and a retiring gentleness that is often the hallmark of British art.

A radically new style of portraiture was introduced by Anthony Van Dyck who settled here in 1632, bringing, from the studio of Rubens via Italy, the full richness of cosmopolitan Baroque painting to the court of Charles I. His unique sensitivity to both national and individual character can be seen in the shimmering grace and relaxed grandeur of 'A Lady of the Spencer Family' which speaks with the kind of eloquence that was to resurface in the work of Gainsborough, Reynolds and Lawrence. The immediate value of Van Dyck's example is shown in the portrait of Endymion Porter by William Dobson, the greatest English-born painter of the century. His style is simpler and more robust; it has neither Van Dyck's distinction nor his hint of melancholy. Dobson adapted the formula of the Continental hunting portrait to produce a convincingly natural image of an English squire at ease with gun and dog. John Michael Wright thirty-five years later used a similar formula in his 'Sir

Neill O'Neill', but here the exotic trappings of an Irish chieftain and some Japanese armour, presumably in Sir Neill's collection, retain the air of theatrical accessories without making a statement about the sitter's personality.

After Van Dyck the development of British painting remained in the hands of foreign artists. In about 1643 Peter Lely brought from Haarlem the weighty, shadowed realism with which he painted his favourite musical subjects. At his best, in portraits like that of the scholar Mercurius Van Helmont, he could express a sensitive but forceful masculinity; his women, however, tend to lose their individuality behind the mask of fashionable beauty. Yet his finest works, such as the 'Two Ladies of the Lake Family', can always be relished for the lovely colour and sumptuous manner he developed for the Restoration court. Lely was the first of the tycoons to dominate the portrait business in Britain, with a studio geared to producing vast numbers of often standardised likenesses and their replicas. His contemporary Gerard Soest was no match for Lely's efficiency, but his 'Lady as a Shepherdess' shows that he commanded a cool and wanton voluptuousness of his own, while his ability to cope with the pomp of the international Baroque state portrait is shown in his 'Duke of Norfolk'. Among British-born painters the flamboyant Isaac Fuller, who had studied in France, was the most natural Baroque talent. John Michael Wright, on the other hand, who had learnt his Baroque style in Rome, continued to place

William Dobson, **Endymion Porter** *c.*1643–5

Sir Peter Lely, **Two Ladies of the Lake Family** *c.*1660

'View of Hampton Court'. In strong contrast, however, is the naturalism and subtle lighting of Jan Siberechts' 'Landscape with Rainbow, Henley on Thames', which anticipates the achievements of the eighteenth century.

Jan Siberechts, **Landscape with Rainbow, Henley on Thames** *c.*1690

more emphasis on individual quirkyness than on the smoothly fashionable, a reflection perhaps of his wider antiquarian and scholarly interests.

Lely was succeeded by the German Godfrey Kneller who was to dominate British portraiture for nearly half a century until his death in 1723. Kneller had a sharp eye for forceful character; he responded with equal perceptiveness to sitters like 'The Marquess of Tweeddale' and to some of the greatest talents of his time, though his good qualities were all too often overwhelmed by the demands of studio mass production.

Towards the end of the seventeenth century the decorative style of the late Baroque was at last naturalised in Britain. Italian and French artists like Verrio and Louis Chéron came to execute grand decorative schemes in the country seats and town houses of the aristocracy, and Chéron became a founder of the St Martin's Lane Academy where Hogarth was to study. Sir James Thornhill, the painter of the Hall at Greenwich and the Cupola of St Paul's, became the British master of the style; he gave its grandeur a quality that was appropriately realistic, almost prosaic.

Animal painting was at this stage still an adjunct of the decorative arts, taking mostly the form of 'overdoors' and 'overmantels'. Its earliest British exponent was Francis Barlow who observed birds, hounds and other animals with a directness and honesty that looks forward to the development of sporting-painting as an independent genre. Still-life, an art form that never really took root in this country, was supplied from the Netherlands by artists like Edward Collier, who may or may not have visited Britain in the last years of the seventeenth century, and who turned out a stream of near-identical still-lifes with texts and emblems to suit both the British and Dutch markets. A similarly low status was occupied by landscape, and the artificiality of most early landscape painting in Britain is typified by the map-like detail, high viewpoint and wayward topography of Jan Griffier's

David Des Granges
The Saltonstall Family *c*.1637
Oil on canvas,
$84\frac{1}{2} \times 108\frac{3}{8}$ (214.2 × 275.5)

This unique family scene can be dated to the last years of the 1630s on grounds of dress, and is attributed to David Des Granges, who is chiefly known as a miniature painter but who also painted life-size subjects entirely compatible in style with this. His somewhat provincial style is admirably suited to cope with a subject that is not only a family portrait but also a dynastic record of family events, closest in feeling to the massive family church monuments fashionable at the time.

The picture shows Sir Richard Saltonstall of Chipping Warden at the bedside of his first wife, who died in 1630. She is shown on her death-bed, noticeably pale, pointing with a tender gesture to her two surviving children, a boy and a girl. The lady seated in the chair beside her is Sir Richard's second wife whom he married in 1633; she holds their first child, which suggests that the picture was painted around 1637. This imaginative gathering of the family in one portrait defies the increasing taste for naturalism prevalent at the time, and harks back to an Eliza-bethan mentality in its desire to record genealogical fact, as it does in its cheerful insistence on patterning and flat bright colours. At the same time the work has a sensitive, intro-spective quality and a certain relaxed gracefulness that shows an aware-ness of Van Dyck and particularly Cornelius Johnson. Above all, the subtle psychological relationships suggested between the sitters, expressed in the linked hands of the group on the left, the husband's gentle drawing back of the bed curtain, his first wife's answering gesture and Sir Richard's glance at his new wife and child (drawing them into the group while allowing them to remain as if unaware of the 'history' behind them) makes this a work of remarkable tenderness and charm.

The painting comes from Wroxton Abbey, Oxfordshire, a seat of the North family, among whose ancestors the Saltonstalls were.

The Early Eighteenth Century

James Seymour, **A Kill at Ashdown Park** 1743

With the accession of George I in 1714 Britain embarked on a long period of peace and economic prosperity that was reflected in the increasing wealth of the bourgeoisie. There was now scope for a less aristocratic taste in painting. Narrative painting, which was eventually to assume such a dominating role in the nineteenth century, began on a literary, illustrative level with such works as the 'Hudibras' series attributed to Francis Le Piper, who is known to have illustrated Butler's famous anti-Puritan satire; it was also to become one of Hogarth's earliest subjects. Portrait painters like John Vanderbank also ventured into the genre, and his many small oils illustrating the story of 'Don Quixote' anticipate, at a much less controlled level, Hogarth's emphatic and free use of paint. Joseph Highmore's illustrations of 1745 to the bestseller of the century, his friend Richardson's sentimental novel *Pamela*, brought the style to a new peak, while Hogarth's 'novels in paint' – his narrative series – created a new art-form altogether by making the genre independent of any literary source.

The Dutch subject of elegant company in an interior added a new dimension to the British concern for portraiture, and examples like that of Peter Angelles, who came to England in about 1715, gave birth to the most cherished of native genres, the conversation piece. Joseph Van Aken, the painter of 'An English Family at Tea', which dates from about five years later, also came from Flanders, but the delicate gravity of the picture was the mood of British painting at the time. At a more boisterous level the subject was continued in the interiors with merry company of Marcellus Laroon. The taste for French elegance began to manifest itself in this country in the 1720s, when Philip Mercier arrived from France with a repertoire of genteel domestic genre subjects and a lucrative line in small conversation pieces modelled on the pastorals of Watteau. His 'Music Party', probably painted for a series to illustrate the five senses, is typical of his approach. His coy seamstresses and oyster girls found a ready echo in the attractive but repetitive pin-ups of Henry Morland, and later in the pretty country girls of Francis Wheatley. The conversation piece, a type of portrait comprising two or more full-length figures in an informal setting, need not always be small, but by and large the term has come to be associated with the small-

scale pictures (as distinct from miniatures) which represented the cheaper end of the portrait market. They were also well attuned to the more intimate scale of the Rococo, with the result that the British artists most influenced by the Rococo were also the most successful painters of conversation pieces. At its most recognisable the style appears in the paintings of Francis Hayman. His close collaboration as an illustrator with the superb French designers and engravers working in Britain (engraving was very much a French monopoly in England at this time) left a permanent imprint on him. Although far removed from the rarefied mood of their French counterparts, his small-scale portraits are lively and graceful, and the light palette and feathery touch of pictures like 'The Wrestling Scene' from *As You Like It* show his debt to Gravelot. This Shakespearean scene is probably related to Hayman's decorations for the most notable outburst of the Rococo to occur in England, the public pleasure gardens at Vauxhall, which were opened, redecorated in the new style, in 1732. His large 'See-Saw' is an actual survivor of the innumerable decorative panels which many leading painters of the day executed, mostly to French designs, for the supperboxes there, and it gives a good impression of the gay spirit that prevailed throughout the scheme. Hayman was an important influence on the young Gainsborough and thus probably gave impetus to the French-orientated tendencies of this much greater artist.

Yet once again British taste stiffened the more flamboyant aspects of an imported style, and the prim little figures of Arthur Devis betray little of the original verve of the Rococo, but belong to it by virtue of their delicate charm, soft colouring and overall air of comfortable ease in their parkland and country house settings. Devis was one of the very few painters to devote himself entirely to the conversation piece and, having found his level, to eschew all ambitions as regards the so-called nobler forms of painting. It is perhaps this total lack of bombast that makes his work so appealing now.

Gravelot's lessons in Rococo sensibility were, however, most naturally assimilated, perhaps because of his own gentler nature, by the gifted Joseph Highmore. His illustrations to *Pamela* have none of the satirical bite or intent of his almost exact contemporary Hogarth, and his talent was possibly the clearest expression of the sentimental bourgeois taste of the day. As a portrait painter he was perfectly at home in the bland world of society portraiture, as exemplified in the 'Man in a Brown Coat', which could have been just another eighteenth-century fashion plate had not the painter been able to kindle a wry amusement in his sitter's expression. Highmore displays his real mettle when he can indulge in an affectionate study of character, as when painting himself at ease with a group of friends in the astonishing 'Mr Oldham and his Guests'. So perceptive, full of skill, humour and truthful observation is the picture, that one is not surprised that for a long time it was attributed to Hogarth.

Pictures, in a phrase of the art theorist Richardson, 'are subservient to virtue', and though the practical impact of the academic ordering of the arts into a hierarchy of relative moral importance belongs to the second half of the eighteenth century, moral probity and decorum is the hallmark of portraiture under the Georges from the earliest days. Few manifest this quality more consistently than Thomas Hudson, the most successful portrait painter to span the middle decades of the century. He could respond with sensitivity to agreeable faces as in 'Mrs Collier', but often much of the well-groomed efficiency of his portraits derives from the custom of using professional drapery painters; in fact, Joseph Van Aken's glossy silks and satins are thought to be responsible for a certain sameness that is to be found in a large proportion of London society portraits painted before the middle of the century. This division of labour was usual throughout the century, although Hogarth and Gainsborough are known to have disdained the practice.

A painter of much greater individual gifts was the Scotsman Allan Ramsay, who may be mentioned here, as much of his most mature work was painted before the middle of the century. His study abroad brought to his portraiture both Italian bravura and French gracefulness, which combined happily with a native ability to interpret character with sympathy and forthrightness. Although he worked well into the third quarter of the century, he remained aloof from the Academy and painted nothing but portraits. The high standard that provincial portraiture could achieve is shown in the agreeable directness of the West-countryman George Beare, whose known portraits all date from the 1740s.

One of the most genuinely native types of painting in Britain is the horse picture. The leading exponents of this genre in the first half of the eighteenth century were John Wootton, whose rough and painterly style, particularly in landscape, owed much to Italian models, and James Seymour, whose neat line and apparently naïve vision give a meticulous rendering of fact in which the setting and even the individual dogs are identifiable. Paradoxically, this adherence to truth appears more artificial than Wootton's imaginary Italianate parkland in his portrait of 'Members of the Beaufort Hunt'.

The development of British landscape painting began modestly as an extension of the country house portrait and the sporting picture; at the same time an elevated form of the genre was recognised in the classical landscapes of Claude and Poussin, though their qualities were only superficially understood. One of the first artists to devote himself specifically to landscape painting was George Lambert. His 'View of Box Hill' of 1733 is one of the earliest recorded paintings of the English countryside unencumbered by the motif of a hunt or a country house; his 'Classical Landscape' of 1745, on the other hand, shows his interpretation of a grand style in landscape according to the rules of Poussin. He was also one of the first to take Dutch picturesque landscapes for his models. A purely topographical type of view-painting was practised by another visitor from abroad, Balthasar Nebot, whose view of Covent Garden of 1734 is a straightforward glimpse of London life of the period, while the young Richard Wilson's 'View of the Middle Temple after the Fire of 1737' concentrates on fact and anecdote with little hint as yet of the revolution in British landscape painting he was to effect nearly twenty years later.

Peter Monamy was the first important British marine painter, and though he largely imitated the great Dutch tradition of seascape painting, his 'Ships in Distress' anticipates Turner's stormy sensibility.

Arthur Devis, **The James Family** 1751

Hogarth

William Hogarth, **O the Roast Beef of Old England ('Calais Gate')** 1748

Hogarth was the first of the great painters of the eight-eenth century. He was well aware of his position as a pioneer; above all, he was English and proud of it. His truculent self-confidence marked all his work, but it was linked with a robust humanity and a sensitive empirical vision.

Hogarth was trained as an engraver, and we have no certain knowledge of him as a painter before he was thirty, but there is reason to think that earlier he had painted pictures showing trades and everyday activities, among them the sharply characterised 'Doctor's Visit'. His first success as a painter, the 'Scene from *The Beggar's Opera*', deliberately capitalised on the popu-larity of John Gay's ballad opera in 1728. The several versions that Hogarth painted of it were probably the first British paintings of actual stage scenes and both the choice of subject and delicate handling of paint owe something to French examples. Hogarth pursued the social and moral comment to which the *Beggar's Opera* scene owed much of its success in the four series of 'modern moral subjects' that made him famous. At the Tate this vein is represented by 'O the Roast Beef of Old England ('Calais Gate')', in which the satire is political. Its theme was the poverty and superstition that Hogarth

discovered across the Channel; patriotism and outraged pride gave this satire a special edge. The canvas known as 'The Staymaker', possibly intended for a series on the theme of 'The Happy Marriage', was left in the unfinished state of a sketch; the rhythmic freedom and iridescence of blue and grey reveal the painterly qualities that under-lie such pictures. From 1739 onwards he turned from small-scale portraiture and cabinet pictures to paint for some years chiefly life-size portraits. He took up the tradition of Kneller, again with an admixture of French influence, and developed a robust substance and a directness that give us some of the freshest and most palpable images of people of his time that we possess. One of his grandest performances is 'Archbishop Herring', begun in 1744 with the declared intention of rivalling Van Dyck and Kneller. Rather later he painted the tender and understanding study of the heads of his six servants, a private picture in which sympathy is unmixed with the worldliness of his other portraits.

William Hogarth,
Heads of Six of Hogarth's Servants *c.*1750–5

Hogarth's ambitions always included the desire to outdo the foreign old masters and to be a successful History Painter in the manner of his father-in-law Thornhill, but there was little taste and few opportunities for painting such works. 'Sigismunda' was painted as a challenge to the high price paid for a supposed Correggio in 1759 and it was, predictably, received with ridicule. However, one such picture, the sinister 'Satan, Sin and Death', on a theme from Milton, painted probably be-fore 1740, had an extraordinary originality and must have been connected with the developing theories of the sublimity of terror. Through posthumous engravings this fiery sketch became widely influential in the latter part of the century and marked, in a sense, the beginning of the Romantic movement.

William Hogarth
The Graham Children 1742
Oil on canvas,
$63\frac{1}{4} \times 71\frac{1}{2}$ (160.5 × 181)

One of Hogarth's finest large-scale compositions, this picture shows the children of Daniel Graham, the wealthy apothecary of the Chelsea Hospital. It is an intimate conversation piece rooted in the bourgeois taste of the day, while at the same time inviting comparison with Van Dyck's famous group of the children of Charles I in a manner to please any nouveau-riche. Above all, Hogarth cannot avoid commenting on the human condition and the picture becomes a parable of the passing of time and the vulnerability of innocence. The eldest girl looks at the spectator as though the first to be aware of the outside world. Her brother and sisters still play in the protected world of their childhood as unconcernedly as the bird sings in its cage, mindless of the fascinated cat, just as the children are unaware of the golden infant Time watching from the clock opposite. None of these motifs was invented by

Hogarth, but they represent a remarkably fresh use of symbols long current in Dutch genre painting. The artist has effortlessly combined their use with a beautiful Rococo sense of colour and springiness of line, taking the opportunity to incorporate his beloved S-curve – the 'line of Grace and Beauty' – prominently in the fall of the eldest girl's apron. The elaborate silver bowl of fruit on the floor beside the baby girl is a bravura piece of still-life painting rarely met with in Hogarth's art.

Richard Robert Graham, the boy playing the bird organ, still owned the painting in 1805, and it probably left the family's possession soon after his death in 1816. After changing ownership a few times in the nineteenth century, it was eventually bought from the Normanton collection by Lord Duveen, and presented to the National Gallery in 1934.

The Age of Confidence

Samuel Scott, **An Arch of Westminster Bridge** *c.*1750

During the second half of the eighteenth century British painting achieved a self-confidence that allowed native painters not to stand behind or in opposition to the Continental schools, but to range themselves alongside them. The period is dominated by four outstanding painters – Reynolds, Gainsborough, Wilson and Stubbs – and one cardinal event, the foundation of the Royal Academy in 1768.

Attempts to create a corporate identity among painters in the manner of the older French and Italian academies had begun at the time of Kneller, but none of them achieved the status of a permanent national institution. Venues such as Vauxhall Gardens or the Foundling Hospital, where works by contemporary artists could be seen by the public, were very few. The year 1760 saw not only the accession of George III, but also the first public exhibition of paintings, organised by the new Society of Artists, an amateurish forerunner of the altogether more professional and high-minded Royal Academy. It was the latter that gave artists a completely new relationship to their clients and a new position in society. The epitome of this new status was Sir Joshua Reynolds, its first President, whose annual lectures served as the fountainhead of academic doctrine. Its chief tenet was the hierarchy of different kinds of painting according to subject, each with its own suitable mode of expression, the highest being religious, allegorical and historical subjects painted according to rules established in antiquity and displayed in the classical works of the High Renaissance and seventeenth-century Rome. Reynolds called this the 'Grand' or 'Great' style, while everything else, like the Venetian, Dutch and Flemish schools and subjects that were considered non-intellectual, such as landscape, portraiture and still-life, could be classed at various levels of the less noble 'Ornamental' style. He admitted the existence of a third or 'Characteristic' category, in which a strong artistic personality could develop an individual manner that partook of both other styles, prime examples of this being artists like Rubens, Poussin and Salvator Rosa.

Topographical art or view-painting was the least affected by this theorising and continued serenely in the style established in the early eighteenth century, reaching a peak of international excellence with the arrival of Canaletto in London in 1746. By the time he left in 1755, his sparkling views of the great buildings and panoramas of London and the Thames had created a fashion and a demand that native painters could strive to satisfy. Chief among these was Samuel Scott, whose accomplished early work as a marine painter really belongs to the previous chapter. It can be seen at its best in the sense of drama and the brooding tone he achieved in 'Admiral Anson's Action off Cape Finisterre', painted in 1749. After Canaletto's arrival, however, Scott abandoned marine painting almost entirely for Thames and London views in which he showed his understanding of the English atmosphere in a way that makes him the first undisputed English master of the genre. His masterpiece is the 'Arch of Westminster Bridge', a composition in which a solemn grandeur and sense of place fully compensates for a certain lack of that sheer technical brilliance that Canaletto was able to bring to the same subject.

The real revolution in landscape painting was brought about by Richard Wilson. When he departed for Italy in 1749, he was well on the way to becoming a successful portrait painter with a side-line in lively topographical paintings. He was to remain abroad for seven years, and under the impact of the work of the great classical landscape painters Claude and Poussin, his contemporaries Zuccarelli and Vernet, and no doubt the clear light of Italy itself, he soon resolved to devote himself entirely to landscape painting in the grand manner. The difference between Wilson and earlier landscape painters like Lambert and Wootton, who had used classical formulas mechanically, was that he was the first to understand landscape as an elevated and independent form of art, capable of being charged with dramatic or poetic emotion in the manner of History Painting. The serene and expansive 'View of Rome', painted around 1753 for Lord Dartmouth, stands practically at the beginning of this conversion. It shows a profound and creative assimilation of the works of Claude, combined with Wilson's own peculiar understanding of light and mass. A deliberately elegaic note is added to what is essentially a contemporary view by the picturesque fragments of antique sculpture in the foreground, interspersed with figures that could belong to any age. From then on Wilson continued to acquire a repertoire of subjects, of which 'Hadrian's Villa' and 'View of the Campagna' are particularly good examples, which he was able to use as elements in classical compositions for the rest of his life. His greatest and most original contribution was to apply the great traditions of landscape painting to the British, and more particularly to his native Welsh, landscape. He was never able to make his vision of landscape as high art popularly acceptable, though his influence as a teacher was considerable. His pupil and fellow-Welshman Thomas Jones followed his style closely, but without Wilson's dedication or superior painterly gifts, although his brilliant private sketches of Italian buildings show a remarkably fresh and original vision. William Marlow, who was a pupil of Scott as well as of Wilson, produced softer-toned landscapes and town and river views in which both their styles met.

The conversation piece, meanwhile, had moved a long way from the doll-like figures of Devis, and the genre was dominated by the remarkable dexterity of the Austrian Johan Zoffany, who had settled in London in the early 1760s. His meticulous technique had none of the wistfulness and touching charm of the more provincial practitioners. Strong drawing, bright colours and a faithful rendering of faces and objects that left nothing to the imagination made him popular with both the Royal family and the gentry. He was a friend of Garrick, and in his hands the theatrical conversation piece reached a new excellence. Not all his work was confined to the small scale, and on rare occasions he would turn out grand full-

Francis Cotes, **Paul Sandby** 1761

lengths that could rival the neo-classical compositions of Reynolds; one of the best of these is the portrait of Mrs Wodhull, painted in the 1770s. His pupil Francis Wheatley had technically a less firm grasp of his subjects, but greater variety of feeling. His work developed from small-scale conversation pieces of the 1760s, with their cool and reticent approach, to a more sentimental style later. The charge of sentimentality can never be laid at the door of another of Zoffany's pupils, the East Anglian Henry Walton, whose rare subject pictures bring a quiet introspection to bear on their theme that is almost Chardinesque – a quality well displayed in his 'Girl plucking a Turkey'. Small portrait groups full of interest and character were also produced by Mortimer, who will be met with again under the heading of Sublime art. In large-scale portraiture an elegant Anglo-French style was developed by Francis Cotes, who until the 1760s was chiefly a pastellist, but later turned increasingly to oils. His natural gracefulness of line and touch is well demonstrated in his portrait of the landscape painter Thomas Sandby, in a manner entirely worthy of a contemporary of Gainsborough.

The only truly original landscape artist of the period was also one of its greatest portrait painters, Thomas Gainsborough. No other painter applied himself so successfully to both branches of art, though he said that he preferred landscape and only painted portraits for

Richard Wilson, **Rome: St Peter's and the Vatican from the Janiculum** c.1753

Thomas Gainsborough, **The Artist's Daughter Mary** 1777

better likenesses than Reynolds, and portrayed his sitters in a more relaxed manner. In his last ten years, partly under the influence of Murillo, he extracted the genre elements from his landscapes and enlarged them into life-size fancy pictures such as the unfinished 'House-maid'. His unusual talents were brought out by unusual sitters, and his enchanting portrait of the ballerina Giovanna Baccelli, painted for her patron the 3rd Duke of Dorset, is one of the masterpieces of his late period. The same kind of feeling for feminine grace is shown in his more private paintings, like the portraits of his daughters Margaret and Mary. His ability to regard all creatures with unaffected sympathy extended to a subject that Reynolds, for one, would never have associated himself with – the painting of animals. Gainsborough had a countryman's love of dogs, which frequently enter into his portraits in a completely natural way; his 'Pomeranian Bitch and Puppy' is a particularly happy example of his ability to raise them to the level of artistic portraiture. Gainsborough's strength lay in his free and excellent drawing, and many of his paintings give the feeling of the artist thinking with his brush, an immediacy usually reserved for watercolours. It is not surprising that the solemn rulings of the Academy proved unsympathetic to his individual and unrhetorical art, so that in his last years he dissociated himself from it and showed his work only in his studio. His particular talent could leave no successors, and although there were some imitators of his early landscapes – notably Thomas Barker of

a living. He was the kind of painter who paints as if by nature. His works have neither the solidity nor the eclectic resourcefulness of Reynolds, and their substance seems often to depend simply on the fluent and lyrical movement of his brush. Unimpressed by the classical masters (he never went to Italy), he turned to two other sources nearer at hand: Dutch landscapes, which were closely attuned to his native East Anglia, and French sensibility, acquired in the circle of Hayman. The first, combined with the detailed observation of nature, can be seen in his early 'Landscape with a Cornfield', the second in more fanciful works like the 'Landscape with Gypsies'. After he moved to Bath in 1759, and subsequently to London in 1774, the influence of Ruisdael was supplanted by that of another unacademic painter, Rubens, and he painted imaginative landscapes with rustic accessories. Here a sophisticated rhythm of composition and handling replaced the early fresh naturalism which was not to reappear in English art until Constable. Thus his 'Market Cart', painted only a couple of years before his death, shows no trace of the Dutch manner, in which landscape emerges from the careful assemblage of countless small shapes, but is the evocation of the movement of leaves, mass, and light filtered through air, with all the economy of means of a painter who has learnt to think in broad effects. At the same time he made a close study of Van Dyck, and his later portraits show the same diffused light and feathery touch. He had a reputation for catching

Thomas Gainsborough, **The Market Cart** 1786–7

Thomas Gainsborough
Sir Benjamin Truman
Oil on canvas,
$93\frac{5}{8} \times 59\frac{1}{2}$ (237.8 × 151.3)

Gainsborough probably painted this portrait while still living in Bath, not long before he moved to London in 1774. Sir Benjamin Truman was at this time about sixty, the head of one of the largest industrial enterprises in Britain in the second half of the eighteenth century – the brewery which first gained national fame under his direction, and which continues to flourish today. He was knighted on the accession of George III in recognition of his standing in the London business community, and something of his character can be gleaned from his comment to his grandson, written in 1775: 'there can be no other way of raising a great Fortune than by carrying on an Extensive trade. I must tell you Young Man, this is not to be obtained without Spirrit and great Application'. Gainsborough's success in capturing this determined attitude resulted in one of his most impressive male full-lengths. Its pristine condition allows one to appreciate the artist's marvellously free brushwork; no part of the picture is overworked, and with this remarkable economy of means the painting achieves a sense of lightness that in no way skimps the details. The broad harmonies of the greens, browns and yellows combine in an effect of mellow richness, while all the details, from the ageing, forceful face, to the maker's mark inside the hat, are lovingly observed. The landscape background is a compromise that Gainsborough developed at this period between the natural rural English landscape he loved to paint and the artificial backdrop which his more aristocratic sitters found acceptable in grand full-lengths of themselves. It is not the view of a definite place, like the background of the earlier 'Mr and Mrs Andrews' in the National Gallery, but a true pastoral that adds the feel of country breezes and the sound of running water to the solid presence of the man, and creates a sense of space that underlines his self-reliant stance.

Bath – his only pupil and studio assistant was his nephew Gainsborough Dupont, who after his uncle's death continued to work in a manner feebly imitative of him.

George Stubbs was another of the powerful artistic personalities of the period who stood somewhat apart from the Academy, for the simple reason that he was regarded as a mere horse-painter and sporting art was admitted only on sufferance. Yet Stubbs brought a new dimension to the genre, and was not only the greatest master of sporting art, but simply one of the greatest of all British artists. He painted not only horses but all living things with a passionate eye for truth that transcends fashion and conventions. To this he added a sense of artistic harmony and effortless composition that invites musical comparisons. The range of his work extends from idyllic scenes of mares and foals to the dramatically imagined 'Horse frightened by a Lion', from rustic scenes to conversation pictures, and his researches from intensive anatomical studies, including dissection, to such technical experiments as painting in enamel on metal and ceramics. He was the only British artist who approached painting not through academic art training but through the practical study of anatomy. He did go to Italy, but claimed that it confirmed his belief

George Stubbs, **Reapers** 1785

that nature was superior to art. He had no feeling for the grand style, and his attempts to adapt his art to the requirements of History Painting are among his least convincing works. He is, however, without rival in subjects like the 'Haymakers' and 'Reapers', where two kinds of mundane rural activity are interpreted in terms of complex rhythms that weave in and out among the figures, combined with a monumental repose in the composition as a whole and a total lack of any hint of sentimentality. A similar play of tensions between shapes and masses is set up in the deceptively simple 'Hound and Bitch in a Landscape'.

The most dominant force in British painting of the period was, however, Sir Joshua Reynolds. He imposed his image on the whole age, and it is he who, so to speak, gives us the official portrait of the eighteenth century. He set out with great deliberation to achieve this. In 1740 he was apprenticed to the fashionable Hudson, but even his early portraits show a preoccupation with light and shade and a free handling of paint that went beyond what Hudson's studio and the pedestrian mid-eighteenth century style could offer. He was unique among British painters in his concern with artistic theory, and it is this,

Sir Joshua Reynolds, **Admiral Viscount Keppel** 1780

combined with a burning ambition to excel and a remarkable eye for the real shape of things, which allowed him to tower over his contemporaries. There is no such thing as a Reynolds face, in the way there is a Hudson or a Devis face, for with few painters has one so consistently the feeling that each sitter was met as a fresh problem to be solved in a different and often novel way, rather than moulded into a fashionable norm. This was because for Reynolds the norm to strive for was not the fashionable, but the ideal. When he returned from Italy in 1752 he had absorbed and understood the lessons of the High Renaissance more deeply than any British artist before him, and it was his ambition to link a British school of painting to this tradition. His other aim was to raise the status of the painter to that of a scholar and thinker. His talents were appreciated almost immediately, and by the time the Royal Academy came to be founded in 1768,

George Stubbs
Mares and Foals in a Landscape
*c.*1762–8
Oil on canvas,
40 × 63¾ (102 × 162)

Stubbs' compositions of brood mares and foals, of which there are at least nine, mostly dating from the 1760s, form an important part of the artist's work. Not only do they represent a splendid artistic monument to the English enthusiasm for horsebreeding, but they are also one of the purest expressions of Stubbs' remarkable control of line and shape. We know from an unfinished picture in the series that Stubbs first painted the horses in perfect detail, stretching them across a blank background like the figures in a classical frieze, and then the landscape would be carefully inserted into the background and between the legs. The resulting combination of Stubbs' passionate concern for anatomical accuracy, the harmony of the flowing design with which the individual shapes are made to relate to each other, and the dreamy, probably purely imaginary landscape, represents one of the most compelling images in British art. This rhythmic quality, often expressed in slow curves that arise out of the natural outlines of the horses, endows Stubbs' work with a poetry and sometimes a sense of strangeness that lifts it well above the level of ordinary sporting art. At the same time the pictures are accurate portraits of specific mares, famous either for success on the turf, or as the dams of winners, painted with a truth to nature that enables experts to tell that they are thoroughbreds that represent an advance on their purely Arabian ancestors.

The painting was for several generations in the collection of the Earls of Middleton, but its early history and the exact circumstances of its commission are not known.

Reynolds' position as the leading British painter made his appointment as its first President inevitable. Apart from his success in establishing a tradition of objective art criticism, his great merit as a painter was to enlarge vastly the scope of the only commercially viable branch of painting in Britain – portraiture – by linking it to the grand style. He achieved this through his immensely wide reference to the old masters, from whom he could 'quote' at will, in a manner he felt most suitable to his sitter. Not all attempts were successful, and the method frequently led to an overblown presentation of his sitters which we find unsympathetic today. Yet the weight and distinction of Reynolds' portraits completely eclipsed the work of his predecessors like Hudson, or even the often more subtle Allan Ramsay. Whether modelling his 'Lady Bampfylde' on the Medici Venus, or a child's portrait on Raphael's angels, or representing the digni-fied age of his friend Admiral Keppel with uttermost simplicity, the keynote of his works is an openness to the possibilities of each sitter in a way that could enhance what he called 'the mental part' of a picture. Something of the complexity of the man can be glimpsed in the self-conscious and vulnerable nature revealed in his self-portraits. They owe a good deal to Rembrandt, and their serious dignity is not unworthy of the comparison.

One of the rare occasions when British artists have been at the forefront of an international movement was the neo-classical revival that took place in the later 1750s and 1760s. The theorist of this movement was the German Winckelmann, but a pioneer part was played

Benjamin West, **Cleombrotus ordered into Banishment by Leonidas II, King of Sparta** 1768

by Gavin Hamilton and Benjamin West. They painted elevated subjects in a style, based on the antique of Poussin, that anticipated by some twenty years the approach of Jacques-Louis David, with whom one norm-ally associates the high tide of the neo-classical move-ment. While Hamilton stayed in Rome, dealing in anti-quities and painting subjects from Homer, the American-born West settled in England in 1763 and soon supple-mented his themes with subjects taken from the legends of the Middle Ages and recent history. His 'Cleombrotus ordered into Banishment by Leonidas II, King of Sparta' shows the neo-classical style at its purest, but in his later works, such as the sensitive 'Golden Age', he transformed his style into something far more individual. He became the favourite painter of George III and President of the Royal Academy after Reynolds. His portraiture tended to lack depth and was largely a distant imitation of Mengs. He can be regarded as one of the few painters of his age to achieve material success chiefly through History Painting. West's elevation of current events to History Painting was carried further by another American, John Singleton Copley, who established himself in England in 1775 after producing a series of finely characterised portraits that transformed the rather derivative and primitive American tradition. 'The Death of Major Peirson', exhibited in rivalry to the Academy in 1784, drew the public with the appeal of its subject, an incident of only three years before; it is treated as a composition in the grand manner and painted crisply, in cool, fresh colours. The same characteristics can be found in George Romney, who, after Gainsborough and Reynolds, had the largest share of the portrait prac-tice in London. He had neither the inventive genius of the latter nor the outstanding gifts of the former, but his understanding of the purity of classical line and cool colouring come nearer to the neo-classical ideal than the

George Romney, **Lady Hamilton as Circe** c.1782

Sir Joshua Reynolds
**Three Ladies Adorning a Term
of Hymen** 1774
Oil on canvas,
$92 \times 114\frac{1}{2}$ (233.7 × 290.8)

This portrait of the three Montgomery sisters epitomises the kind of painting, known as the Grand style, which was established in Britain by Reynolds and dominated the latter part of the eighteenth century. From the point of view of an artist whose ambition it was to raise portraiture to the status of History Painting, this was an ideal commission. The Right Hon. Luke Gardiner, fiancé of one of the three girls, requested in 1773 that Reynolds should compose for him a picture of the three sisters 'in full length, representing some emblematic or historical subject', selected according to his 'genius and poetic invention'. Reynolds chose the subject of a rite of worship to the God of Wedlock as being both suitable to the occasion and at the same time representing a self-sufficient theme taken from Poussin and the classics, with echoes of Rubens' 'Nature attired by the Three Graces' thrown in for good measure. This was the public façade of the picture, designed to be appreciated by the educated connoisseur and to flatter the sitters by placing them among the immortals. A more private dimension was meant to be understood by the family: Ann, the youngest of the sisters and the first to be married, is shown having passed the image of Hymen; Mrs Gardiner, the second to marry, is shown, so to speak, at the post, while the eldest, not to be married for another year, is still collecting flowers for the rite. The attitudes borrowed from various, mostly Italian, sources were then adapted and transformed by Reynolds into a graceful rising chain of movement, while the strong contrasts in light and shade give the composition weight and stability. The result represents in practice Reynolds' ardently held theory that contemporary art should be blended with the classical in order to approach more closely a timeless ideal.

Joseph Wright, **Experiment with the Air-pump**
exhibited 1768

John Singleton Copley, **The Death of Major Peirson,
6 January 1781** 1783

The range of painting was also being expanded by the development of other more peculiarly English types of subjects. Joseph Wright of Derby combined an interest in contrasted effects of light, derived from the Dutch tenebrists, with a fascination for industrial and scientific subjects. The scale of his masterly 'Experiment with an Air-pump', painted in 1767–8, rightly implied a claim to the status of History Painting. In his portraits he avoided the grand manner of Reynolds as much as the seductive grace of Gainsborough; his portrait of Sir Brooke Boothby of 1780–1 consciously stresses, through the volume of Rousseau held by the sitter, the new cult of nature.

While Hoppner and Northcote followed in the footsteps of Reynolds, the closing decades of the century saw the rise of two outstanding new masters of portrait painting, Raeburn and Lawrence. Raeburn worked practically all his life in Scotland, and his obsession with light and a powerful, individual handling of paint resulted in a genuine development of Reynolds' grand style that carried it without loss of conviction into the early nineteenth century. Reynolds' late style was, however, most brilliantly adapted by the precocious Thomas Lawrence. He lacked Reynolds' intellectual cast of mind

work of any of the other contemporary portrait painters. Like so many others, he fancied himself primarily as a History Painter, and Emma Hamilton's 'attitudes' – classical sculpture come alive, as it were – were his primary inspiration. His 'Lady Hamilton as Circe' exemplifies this vein, although the delightfully fresh 'Parson's Daughter' shows that he was as much captivated by simple health and sheer good looks as by classical features. But the broad planes of his draperies and the generalised beauty of his sitters do capture something of the serenity of classical sculpture, and he can be justly classed as one of the chief exponents of British neoclassicism. Angelica Kaufmann can, as a founder member of the Royal Academy, count as a member of the British school; her feminine version of a soft kind of neoclassicism was more directly inspired by Winckelmann, and her international success showed that the style found a genuine response in popular taste.

Sir Henry Raeburn, **Mrs Downey**

and, after a brief flirtation with History Painting in the form of 'Homer reciting his Poems', painted in 1791 as a twenty-year-old to impress the Academy, he recognised that his strength lay in society portraiture. His 'Kemble as Hamlet' of 1801 unites the tradition of the history and stage portrait in a striking image that is one of the masterpieces of Romanticism. The assurance of his touch comes out well in his sketch for the portrait of Princess Lieven. His best portraits have a restless sparkle and theatrical facility that was in harmony with the Byronic spirit of post-Napoleonic Europe, and with him British portraiture once again achieved international status.

On a minor scale, the tradition of rustic genre established by Gainsborough assumed a less dreamy and more bucolic character in the Dutch-inspired farmyard scenes of George Morland, although well-knit little scenes like 'The Tea Garden' show that he could still command the balanced design and cool decorum of the eighteenth century. The light touch and silvery tonality of Julius Caesar Ibbetson owe much both to the genius of Gainsborough and to the professionalism of Philip James de Loutherbourg, whose close involvement with theatre scenery painting and amazing facility enabled him to produce both softly imaginative landscapes and fierce dramatisations of nature that were to influence the young Turner.

George Morland, **The Tea Garden** engraved 1790

Sir Thomas Lawrence, **Princess Lieven** ?1812–20

The Sublime and the Exotic

In 1757 the philosopher Edmund Burke published his theory of the sublime, which he believed was not simply a degree of beauty, but a quality that was different from conventional beauty. A sublime work of art had to have the power to amaze, astonish, shock and horrify; in his own words, the sublime should 'excite pain or danger' and produce in the spectator 'the strongest emotions which the mind is capable of feeling'. A subject for painting which Burke particularly recommended as sublime was the scene from Milton's *Paradise Lost* where Satan, Sin and Death meet at the gates of Hell. Hogarth, surprisingly, was the first artist to have depicted this

John Hamilton Mortimer, **Sir Arthegal, the Knight of Justice, with Talus, the Iron Man (from Spenser's Faerie Queene)** exhibited 1778

scene, but he was followed by several later artists such as Romney, Barry, West and Blake. Also in 1757, Thomas Gray published his poem *The Bard*, based on the now discredited tradition that Edward I ordered the massacre of all the Welsh bards. The climax of Gray's narrative occurs when the last surviving bard mounts a high peak from which he curses the King before throwing himself into the river below. Painters saw in this episode the purest example of the sublime, and 'The Bard' became one of the most common subjects in late eighteenth- and early nineteenth-century painting, inspiring artists as diverse as Paul Sandby, Thomas Jones, de Loutherbourg, Blake, Fuseli, Turner and John Martin. What must have been the most ambitious treatment of the subject was Benjamin West's eight by six foot canvas, for which the Tate owns what is probably an early oil sketch. West closely followed Gray's description of the bard, especially the long flowing hair and beard.

Fuseli had a perfect background for a painter of the sublime: he was born in Switzerland and was brought up in the intellectual atmosphere of the German 'Sturm and Drang' (storm and stress) movement. His subjects are predominantly horrific, as in 'Lady Macbeth seizing the Daggers', fantastic, as in 'Titania and Bottom', or both, as in the subject he invented for himself, 'Percival delivering Belisane from the Enchantment of Urma'. Fuseli's painting of Lady Macbeth, like so much of his work, is highly individualistic; although the figures are actors – David Garrick and Mrs Pritchard – they are transformed almost completely by Fuseli into ghosts, Macbeth being a transparent and skeletal figure, and Lady Macbeth an apparition swathed in gauzy fabric less like real material than like ectoplasm. It is typical of Fuseli's imagination that the picture is almost colourless save for the red of the blood which stains Macbeth's hands and drips from the daggers.

A splendid example of how the sublime added a new dimension to neo-classical History Painting is John Hamilton Mortimer's imposing canvas of 'Sir Arthegal the Knight of Justice, with Talus, the Iron Man'. The life-size figure of the knight challenges the spectator by his powerful physique, his swashbuckling personality, and his proud possession of the invincible sword which Jupiter himself had once used. Although Mortimer was called the English Salvator Rosa, his hectic and occasionally dissipated life and personality have more in common with Caravaggio, and images such as that of 'Sir Arthegal' even anticipate the full-blooded Romanticism of the age of Byron. Similar use of large figures and dramatic setting is made by James Barry in 'King Lear weeping over the Dead Body of Cordelia'. In the eighteenth century, Shakespeare's play was rewritten to conform to the Age of Reason and given a happier ending in which Cordelia is spared such an unreasonable death. But Barry spares us nothing, and concentrates our attention

Henry Fuseli
Titania and Bottom 1780–90
Oil on canvas,
$85\frac{1}{2} \times 108\frac{1}{2}$ (216 × 275.6)

This extraordinary fantasy is one of Fuseli's many illustrations to Shakespeare's works, and the second picture he produced for the 'Shakespeare Gallery' promoted by Boydell. Fuseli is illustrating Titania's entreaty to Bottom in *A Midsummer Night's Dream*: 'Come, sit thee down upon this flowery bed,/While I thy amiable cheeks do coy'. The artist successfully conveys the coarse grossness of the weaver 'translated' with an ass's head, and the strange beauty of the fairy queen. But it is in Titania's entourage that Fuseli gives his curious imagination its fullest expression. The fairies, some dressed in extravagant and erotic adaptations of contemporary fashionable dress,

some freakish and unnatural, create a sinister atmosphere of evil rather than the pleasantly dreamy mood of Shakespeare's play. In the light of his other work, perhaps Fuseli simply took the opportunity given him by this supernatural subject to exercise his highly personal imagination, or it may be that he discerned the darker side of *A Midsummer Night's Dream* on which modern critics have commented. One of the artist's obsessive themes, that of woman's dominance over man, which in Fuseli's work often takes on a frankly sado-masochistic character, is emphasised here not only in the principal central group, but more particularly in the tall figure on the right leading her dwarfish pet wizard on a leash. This figure unnerves the spectator still further by glancing knowingly out of the picture. The group on the left is even more

bizarre, composed of artificially created, hybrid beings, one with the head of a butterfly. Most of these figures are inventions of Fuseli rather than of Shakespeare, but the artist does include the fairies Peaseblossom (who is scratching the ass's head), Mustard-seed (the tiny figure standing in the palm of Bottom's hand), and, on the right, Cobweb, who kills a bee in order to steal the honey-bag. As well as these principal 'actors', the scene is populated with other aberrations of irrational nature, dimly visible, tiny half-formed creatures who could have crawled out of a picture by Hieronymous Bosch. One of Fuseli's most important paintings, 'Titania and Bottom' displays to the full the peculiar power of his art, and reveals that impulse in certain early Romantic artists to search the nightmare world of the unconscious.

on the God-like figure of Lear – who physically resembles West's Bard – holding the lifeless body of his daughter, while the bleak landscape and stormy sky behind serve to enhance the narrative by visually expressing the distraught state of Lear's mind.

Even before Burke formulated his theory of the sublime, landscape painters – and travellers – had discovered the potentially thrilling qualities of nature's more violent and destructive moods. De Loutherbourg's 'Travellers attacked by Banditti', for example, shows a violent episode of robbery in the wild setting of the mountains. It is rather more than a purely invented scene, because it records a real danger that faced the tourist travelling to Italy. This kind of picture usually conveyed an atmosphere of danger and excitement through the landscape setting of fearsome rocks and blasted trees as well as the action of the figures. This alliance of action and setting owed much to the seventeenth-century paintings of Italian bandits by Salvator Rosa, an artist much admired in eighteenth-century England and whose view of nature was entirely different from the tranquil Arcadia of Claude. De Loutherbourg's 'An Avalanche in the Alps' presents an equal degree of realism; despite the theatrical lighting effects and the melodramatic gestures of the figures in the foreground (which are both reminders of de Loutherbourg's work as a designer for the stage) the turbulent drama of the avalanche is expressed with both forceful immediacy and conviction. The avalanche, along with the storm and the shipwreck, fulfilled most of the qualifications of the sublime, and also visually reflected the unstable state of mind of the later eighteenth-century Man of Feeling. These images were to be yet more potent for the nineteenth-century Romantic artist such as Turner.

Some British artists journeyed further afield than Europe, even in some cases to China and India. William Hodges, for example, a pupil of Richard Wilson, went as draughtsman with Captain Cook to the Antarctic and with Warren Hastings to India. It was in India in 1782 that he painted the landscape identified as a tomb with the distant hills of Rajmahal. The picture is primarily a topographical view, but Hodges gives it the Claudian sense of order and control that he had learned from his master Wilson; the most Indian feature of the painting is the architecture of the tomb itself. A more extensive topographical sketching tour was undertaken in India by Thomas Daniell and his nephew William, a tour which provided several subjects for painting after their return to England. One such painting is 'Sher Shah's Mausoleum, Sasaram', worked up from a direct transcription of the monument of the kind the Daniells used for their *Oriental Scenery*, plates which familiarised the English with Indian architecture and contributed to the most spectacular use of its forms and motifs in the Royal Pavilion at Brighton.

Thomas Daniell, **Idgah at Amroha** 1810

Philip James de Loutherbourg,
An Avalanche in the Alps 1803

Blake and his Followers

William Blake, **The Penance of Jane Shore in St Paul's Church** ?c.1793

William Blake is one of the great originals of British art, both as a painter and as a poet. His work stands out in strong contrast to the rational order of the eighteenth century and was a conscious reaction against it: the large colour-print 'Newton' is an allegory of the limited vision of the rational man uninspired by the imagination. Nevertheless much of his work reflects interests widespread at the time. Some of his early designs were essays in neo-classical History Painting; he illustrated Gray's poems and several of the fashionable moralisings on mortality; his use of Gothic forms derived from his apprenticeship to Thomas Basire for whom he worked in Westminster Abbey in connection with publications that ministered to the new taste for British antiquities; many of his other images were influenced by the Old Master engravings he saw during his apprenticeship and when joint-owner of a print-shop. He read widely, especially among mystical writers such as Paracelsus, Swedenborg, Böhme and the neo-Platonists as introduced into England through the translations of Thomas Taylor, yet the main influence on his writings and imagery was the literary tradition of the England in which he grew up, the Bible, Milton and Shakespeare.

Blake's first works are largely in the current neo-classical idiom, as can be seen by comparing 'The Penance of Jane Shore', a later, more accomplished version of a watercolour of about 1779–80, with Benjamin West's 'Cleombrotus' of 1768. This neo-classical influence reached its peak in the mid 1780s, as in 'Oberon, Titania and Puck, with Fairies dancing', but it also lies behind the by then completely personal style, linear and with an emphasis on symmetry, of many of the biblical watercolours of 1800–5.

As in this case, such influences were absorbed into Blake's own vision, which was concerned, both in poetry and painting, with the expression of eternal truths through the 'Poetic Genius'. It is a common fallacy that an artist's creations directly embody his own personal beliefs and philosophy, whereas in fact all sorts of other factors must be taken into account when assessing the independent work of art, but for Blake, at least in his mature works, the art does reflect the man. Blake, who pondered deeply on the problem of good and evil and arrived at an idiosyncratic form of Christianity, embodied his beliefs in what may be described as his own mythology and many of the characters that appear in his writings, such as Los, Urizen and Orc, are either directly represented in his designs or equated there with figures from the Bible, literature or history.

The series of large colour prints of 1795 (the earliest

William Blake, **The Four and Twenty Elders casting their Crowns before the divine Throne** 1805

William Blake, **The Spiritual Form of Pitt guiding Behemoth** ?1805

before Pitt's repressive measures made such openness impossible and contributed towards a turning inwards that produced the despair of the 1795 colour prints.

Blake's illustrations to the Bible of about 1799–1805 are more optimistic, reflecting a growing reconciliation with at least the Christianity of the New Testament. Even late in his life, however, his illustrations to *The Book of Job* and Dante's *Divine Comedy* embody sharp criticism of the orthodox beliefs of the texts. By a strange paradox 'Beatrice addressing Dante from the Car', for all its exquisite handling and glowing colour, represents Blake's attack on Dante's identification of Beatrice as the Church with a positive role in man's salvation.

William Blake, **The Ghost of a Flea** *c.*1819

works to show Blake's full powers and perhaps his greatest achievement) are typical of the way in which his philosophy unified subjects taken from the most disparate sources: as well as the Bible the prints draw on Milton ('The House of Death' from *Paradise Lost*), Shakespeare ('Pity' from the lines in *Macbeth*), his own mythology ('The Good and Evil Angels', a representation of Los and Orc) and the recent past ('Newton'). They seem to represent Blake's views on the Fall and man's subsequent predicament, which he saw as the consequence of the splitting up of the original unified man into his component elements, imagination, reason, emotions and the senses, which, once divided, struggle against each other. Symbolism such as the worm entwining the newly created being in 'Elohim creating Adam' shows the pessimism with which Blake viewed the Creation, while in 'God judging Adam' he attacked the vengeful God of the Old Testament by likening him to Urizen, Blake's embodiment of the oppressive exercise of the rational will.

Blake's completely unrealistic portrayal of 'Newton' (to show man at his most rational, a counterpart of the biblical 'Nebuchadnezzar', man at his most material) has a parallel in 'The Spiritual Form of Pitt' and 'The Spiritual Form of Nelson', in which he interpreted two leading figures of his age in the light of the Apocalypse. These were shown at his unsuccessful exhibition of 1809 and are a reminder of his earlier years as an active radical,

William Blake, **Beatrice addressing Dante from the Car** 1824–7

William Blake
Elohim creating Adam 1795
Colour print finished in pen and
watercolour,
$17 \times 21\frac{1}{8}$ (43.1 × 53.6)

This is the first of Blake's great series
of large colour prints of 1795, the
culmination of a technique developed in his illuminated books. They
combine printing with direct handling. First Blake would apply his
colours to a flat surface, probably a
sheet of millboard rather than the
copper plates he used for printing his
books. Then he would take a number
of impressions, usually three, on
separate sheets of paper. These
would vary in effect, the first print
being fuller and heavier than the
subsequent ones. All, even the first,
would then be finished in watercolour and, for the outlines and
detailed forms, pen. The results
were designs of exceptional richness
of texture, partly because of the thick

pigments themselves, partly because,
in the process of printing, they
produced a variegated, reticulated
effect. The thick medium used was
very similar to that in his later
tempera paintings and some of the
prints are actually signed by Blake
with the descriptive word 'fresco', a
term also applied to some of the later
temperas. Despite his confusion
between painting in tempera on
panel for easel paintings and
painting on wet plaster ('fresco') for
wall paintings, this represents a
deliberate attempt to recapture the
innocence of early Renaissance
painting.

Blake seems quite deliberately to
have chosen this technique for its
effect rather than as a way in which
he could make easy duplicates of his
designs; there can have been little
if any saving in time by the use of
this technique. As his later friend
Frederick Tatham said, 'This plan
he had recourse to, because he could
vary slightly each impression; and

each having a sort of accidental look,
he could branch out so as to make
each one different.'

This is one of Blake's most awe-
inspiring designs. Even without the
symbolism of the worm that entwines
the newly created Adam, stretched
out on the material earth in the form
of the Crucified, the design itself, its
sombre colouring and heavy technique show that Blake saw the
Creation as a negative act. It shows
the submission of the spiritual man
to material existence, a stage in his
Fall into disparate elements. 'Elohim'
is one of the Hebrew names for God,
the Creator in Genesis, and can also
be translated as 'judges'; he re-
appears again in an equally negative
guise, close to that of Blake's own
character Urizen, in another print in
the series, 'God judging Adam'.
However, the Creation, in so far as it
gives a material form to error, acts as
a first essential step in the recognition, and eventual overthrow, of
that error.

Blake's desire to express his ideas as precisely as possible led in the early years of the nineteenth century to his using clear outlines and flat areas of colour with a minimum of chiaroscuro. To this end he rejected oil paint in favour of watercolour and his own form of tempera ('fresco' as he sometimes called it); his 1809 exhibition was expressly designed to demonstrate his accomplishment in this medium. In the case of his earlier temperas his faith in his medium was misplaced, as they have frequently darkened and decayed, but in his last years he successfully refined his technique, as in 'Satan smiting Job with Sore Boils'. At the same time his handling of watercolour, for instance in his illustrations to Dante, became a vehicle of exquisite subtlety and glowing colour, while his engravings to *The Book of Job* achieved a similar sensuous refinement. The special texture of the 1795 colour prints was the result of experiments made in his illuminated books, represented in the Tate Gallery by separate designs from *Visions of the Daughters of Albion* and *Urizen*.

In the last years of his life Blake became the object of veneration among a group of young artists and enthusiasts who called themselves 'The Ancients'. The greatest of these was Samuel Palmer who, inspired by Blake's visionary qualities, by the Shoreham Valley in Kent where he lived and by a strong belief in the established rural order under Church and State, produced from about 1824 to 1834 what are probably the most magical pastorals in English art. Palmer's orthodox views being at the farthest possible remove from Blake's radicalism, it is perhaps hardly surprising that he was chiefly inspired stylistically by Blake's exquisite but untypical wood-engravings for Thornton's edition of Virgil.

These same engravings were also the primary inspiration for the early works of Edward Calvert, which date from the same years. Unlike Palmer's works they exhibit a pagan hedonism that, after a stay in Greece in 1844, dwindled into a nostalgic recreation of the simple life of Ancient Greece. George Richmond, in his precociously early temperas, came closest to Blake's typical style (indeed Blake is said to have corrected the drawing of one of the arms in 'Abel the Shepherd') but lacked the inspiration that fired Palmer and Calvert.

Samuel Palmer, **Coming from Evening Church** 1830

George Richmond,
Christ and the Woman of Samaria 1828

Turner

J.M.W. Turner, **The Shipwreck** exhibited 1805

The paintings of J.M.W. Turner are among the outstanding achievements of the nineteenth century. The richness of the Tate Gallery's collection makes it possible to examine his development, and his diversity, in depth. By the terms under which Turner's somewhat ambiguous will was settled after his death the whole contents of his studio, about 300 oils and 19,000 watercolours and drawings, entered the national collection. With the exception of about ten outstanding examples at the National Gallery all the oils belong to the Tate, which also shows a selection from the watercolours now cared for by the British Museum. The collection of Turner's paintings at the Tate includes pictures shown in public (at the annual exhibitions of the Royal Academy and the British Institution or in his own gallery) and those that he kept out of sight in his studio.

Turner's earliest works were watercolours in the eighteenth-century tradition of the topographical 'tinted drawing', in which a preliminary pencil outline determined the subsequent placing of the washes of colour. However, after a group of watercolours in which he surpassed all previous works in this style, he evolved, together with Thomas Girtin and under the influence of J.R. Cozens, a more flexible technique capable of conveying the most subtle impressions and dramatic force. His first oils are sombre in colour, but already reveal his preoccupation with contrasted effects of light and atmospheric effects such as storms and rainbows. These earliest oils show the predominant influences of Wright of Derby and Wilson, but it seems to have been the paintings of de Loutherbourg that encouraged him in his particular interest in the dramatic possibilities of natural phenomena.

At the turn of the century Turner's ambitions led him to emulate the works of the accepted Old Masters, and in a series of large pictures of the next five years or so he painted sea-pieces in the manner of the van der Veldes, Italianate landscapes in the manner of Claude and 'historical' landscapes in the manner of Poussin. These were, so to say, pictures about pictures and also a direct attack on the pre-eminence of the Old Masters, but Turner soon digested the lessons of his predecessors, making their themes his own and treating them in a completely personal manner. He was taking the traditional styles apart and extracting their essence from them.

At the same time, largely through pencil sketches but occasionally through watercolours and even oils, Turner studied from nature, making long tours in connection with the topographical engravings that provided him with financial security even when his paintings outstripped contemporary taste. The group of small sketches on mahogany veneer, painted on the Thames perhaps in 1807, are outstanding examples, almost rivalling Constable in their freshness and directness. A series of larger sketches on canvas of similar subjects together with scenes on the Thames estuary are more directly studies for the finished paintings of English subjects of about 1807 to 1813, which culminated in 'Frosty Morning'.

The diversity of Turner's landscape style, even at this relatively early period, is echoed in his didactic series of engravings, the *Liber Studiorum*, issued in parts between 1807 and 1819. The idea was derived from Claude's *Liber Veritatis*, but whereas that was a checklist of authentic works, Turner's publication was a deliberate demonstration of the range available to the landscape painter, being, in the words of the sub-title, 'Illustrative of Landscape Compositions, viz. Historical, Mountainous, Pastoral, Marine, and Architectural'.

J.M.W. Turner,
The Thames near Walton Bridges *c.*1807

J.M.W. Turner, **Ploughing up Turnips, near Slough ('Windsor')** exhibited 1809

By 1815, the year in which Turner exhibited 'Crossing the Brook', a scene in Devonshire treated so whole-heartedly in the manner of Claude as to look like an Italian view, the forces driving him towards Italy could no longer be ignored. In 1819 he went, his main centres being Venice, Rome and Naples. The clear light and bright colours of Italy overwhelmed him, and though his watercolours, especially those done in Venice, show him using pure colour without the conventional indication of shadows by dark grey or brown tones, his output of finished pictures for the Royal Academy slackened off considerably. However, 'Bay of Baiae', a panoramic land-scape like 'Crossing the Brook' but with a much more fluid and curvilinear composition, set the pattern for a whole series of such landscapes which he continued to paint well into the 1830s.

The 1820s did however show a great advance in the technique of his oil sketches. These show a much greater range, even within individual sketches, between thin washes and a thick impasto which is often scored into by the brush handle or even Turner's thumbnail to suggest details of form. Those done in 1827 while visiting John Nash on the Isle of Wight are particularly remarkable in that the sketches, seven in all, were painted on two rolls of canvas that were only sub-divided into separate compositions well after Turner's death.

A second visit to Rome in 1828–9 resulted in still bolder compositions in pure colour, the sketches on coarse canvas which seem to have been tryouts for larger compositions (one is for the National Gallery's famous 'Ulysses deriding Polyphemus'). These too were painted on two undivided rolls of canvas. Unlike his first visit to Italy, when he devoted his time to pencil sketches and watercolours, on this occasion he produced a number of oil paintings, even exhibiting a small group in Rome,

much to the mystification of most of the viewers. The exhibits included 'Orvieto', 'Medea' and 'Regulus', but Turner worked on them again to give them their present appearance before exhibiting them back in London. On the same visit Turner painted 'Venus reclining', an impression of Titian's 'Venus of Urbino' simplified into light and colour. Turner's interest in figures had already shown itself in a number of sometimes rather playful genre and historical scenes in the earlier 1820s and continued in the late 1820s and earlier 1830s, partly under the influence of Rembrandt: 'Pilate washing his Hands' shows Rembrandt's chiaroscuro treated in terms of rich colour.

J.M.W. Turner, **Crossing the Brook** exhibited 1815

J.M.W. Turner, **The Bay of Baiae, with Apollo and the Sibyl** exhibited 1823

J.M.W. Turner, **Chichester Canal** *c.*1828

Many of Turner's figure paintings are associated with Petworth where, particularly in the years 1828 to 1837, Turner was a frequent guest of the third Earl of Egremont. The series culminated in 'Interior at Petworth', possibly painted under the impact of Egremont's death in 1837, in which the forms are dissolved in an onrush of light. These visits also produced what are perhaps Turner's most idyllic landscapes, the long oblong compositions designed to be set into the panelling of the dining-room at Petworth though replaced a year or two later by the more finished paintings still in the house.

The idyllic, dream-like landscape, often of Venice, represented one side of Turner's late style. The other was the increasingly direct expression of the destructiveness of nature, apparent particularly in some of his seapieces. The force of wind and water was conveyed both by his open, vigorous brushwork and, in many cases, by a revolving vortex-like composition. In the unexhibited pictures these forces were treated in their own right, but in most of his exhibited works (the distinction lessened in his later years) they were expressed through appropriate subjects such as the Deluge or the Angel of the Apocalypse. In some of these pictures Turner used a colour symbolism, partly deriving from Goethe's theories, as in the pair of pictures 'Shade and Darkness – the Evening of the Deluge' and 'Light and Colour – the Morning after the Deluge', exhibited in 1843 with a specific reference to Goethe. These pictures are examples of Turner's experiments with square, octagonal or circular formats in which the vortex composition found its most compact and energetic expression.

Looking at Turner's pictures of the yellow dawn or the red of sunset, one is aware, perhaps for the first time in art, of the isolation of colour in itself. Even his sea-pieces contain flecks of bright unmodulated colour that enliven their at first sight more monochromatic treatment. To extract from the continuous range of light the purity of yellow, blue or red, the hues that command and comprise the rest, required an uncompromising integrity of vision. Turner had precisely 'the disposition to abstractions, to generalizing and classification' that Reynolds regarded as the great glory of the human mind, though in a form that Reynolds would hardly have recognised. Quite early in Turner's career his pictures were already accounted 'among the vagaries of a powerful genius rather than among the representations of nature'.

In certain watercolours he suspended altogether the definition of a specific subject, leaving almost everything in doubt but the positive existence of colour. Many of the exhibited paintings began the same way; the act of defining a particular scene was postponed until the varnishing days when the paintings were already hanging, and then performed with astounding brilliance. By the 1830s, as Charles Eastlake told Turner's first biographer Walter Thornbury, none of Turner's 'exhibited pictures could be said to be finished till he had worked on

J.M.W. Turner, **Interior at Petworth** *c.*1837

them when they were on the walls of the Royal Academy'. Another contemporary artist described how Turner sent in a picture to the British Institution exhibition of 1835 in a state no more finished than 'a mere dab of several colours, and "without form and void"'; the account continues that 'Such a magician, performing his incantations in public, was an object of interest and attraction'. These 'dabs' of several colours must have looked much like, say, 'Norham Castle'. Turner's process of transformation can be seen by comparing a sketch like 'Venice with the Salute' with an exhibited picture such as 'Dogana, San Giorgio Citella, from the Steps of the Europa'.

Yet even in the most private, least-finished pictures there is never that detachment from outward reality that is now called abstract. On the contrary: he evolved with poetic freedom the real quality of the world. In the sumptuous style that reached its height in the mid 1830s, the material of nature was translated into resounding chords of colour. Then, particularly in the pictures that remained in Turner's studio, specific colour gradually dissolved into a general medium of vision, like a bright vapour – the hue of lucent air. There is rarely any doubt about the things represented, but they are formed out of a common elemental medium that washes over and through them.

Turner outgrew theatrical extravagance but the essential sublimity of the forces that hold man in their grip remained with him always. There is a sense of it in the all-embracing flood of light that envelops a scene, and the spectator too. The last subjects of storm and catastrophe make visible a dream of peril and endurance that is full of heroic exaltation. The elemental drama that Turner painted was both real and imaginary.

Many of Turner's most striking innovations appeared first in his watercolours, of which a changing selection is shown at the Tate. In the late unfinished oils like 'Norham Castle' distinctions of medium have disappeared, delicate films of oil paint float transparently over the white ground like washes of watercolour on paper, and the last traces of the eighteenth-century hierarchy of artistic values have been overthrown.

J.M.W. Turner, **Venice with the Salute** c.1840–5

J.M.W. Turner, **The Dogana, San Giorgio, Citella, from the steps of the Europa** exhibited 1842

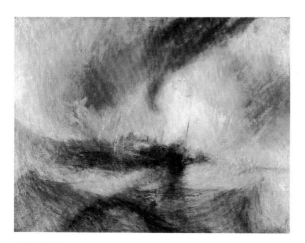

J.M.W. Turner, **Snow Storm: Steam-Boat off a Harbour's Mouth** exhibited 1842

J.M.W. Turner
Norham Castle *c.*1835–40
Oil on canvas, 35¾ × 48 (91 × 122)

Norham Castle on the River Tweed obsessed Turner throughout his career. He first went there on his first tour of the north of England in 1797 when he did a single pencil drawing in his sketchbook. This led to two finished watercolours, one of which was exhibited at the Royal Academy the following year as 'Norham Castle – Summer's Morn', a title that already, this early in Turner's career, typified his interest in the changing effects of the seasons and times of day. A few years later, on his way to Scotland in 1801, Turner made a whole series of pencil sketches of the castle, but no further finished works resulted until about 1815 when he used the subject for one of the plates in his *Liber Studiorum*, a series of engravings published over the years through which Turner demonstrated

the range and variety of his treatment of landscape. About 1822 Turner painted another finished watercolour which was engraved in 1824 for the topographical publication *The Rivers of England*. In 1831 Turner again passed Norham Castle on his way to Scotland, and used it for one of his illustrations to Walter Scott's *The Provincial Antiquities of Scotland*, 1834, 'Norham Castle – Moonrise'.

Besides the finished watercolours and drawings, Turner painted a series of much more abstract 'colour beginnings' of the subject. Two are in watercolour, one probably of about 1817, the other of the mid 1830s. This last was developed in the oil painting in the Tate Gallery, one of a group of very thinly painted 'colour beginnings' in oils in which Turner's work in this medium approached most closely to his watercolour technique. Diluted washes of oil paint were floated over a white ground in a

manner identical to that in which Turner applied thin watercolour washes to white paper. However, the greater flexibility of the oil medium has resulted in areas of crisp, relatively thick paint, almost certainly applied with the palette knife to suggest the glow of light from the sky and the effect of its . falling on the river and its banks below. The castle itself is also fairly thickly painted though in more liquid, rounded strokes, but the miraculous allusiveness of Turner's technique is demonstrated by the fact that elsewhere the solid forms of the landscape are the most thinly painted. Equally revolutionary is Turner's use of colour, suggestive rather than descriptive, with the castle in blue, the cow in red, and the river banks and distant hills in a combination of pearly pinks, delicate blues and pale browns enlivened by yellow and white impasto to suggest the flicker of sunlight.

Constable

John Constable, **Malvern Hall, Warwickshire** 1809

John Constable, **A Lane near Flatford (?)** *c.*1810

Unlike Turner, Constable entered the art world fairly late in life, and he made painfully slow progress once he was in it. Born at East Bergholt, Suffolk, the son of a prosperous corn merchant, John Constable spent several years in the family business before deciding, and obtaining permission, to study painting full-time. Before he went to the Royal Academy schools in 1799 (the same year that Turner, only very slightly older, was elected as an Associate) he had acquired some sort of grounding however: his spare time had been passed with the local plumber and artist, John Dunthorne; he had been intro-

duced to the connoisseur Sir George Beaumont and had been shown his Claude 'Hagar and the Angel'; and he had made friends with two artists-cum-antiquarians, John Cranch and J. T. Smith, assisting the latter with his etchings of picturesque cottages and with his research on Gainsborough. Once in London, Constable studied Old Master landscapes in the collections of Beaumont, Beckford and the influential Academician Joseph Farington. Constable continued to study and copy the work of his predecessors for as long as he lived, constantly measuring their interpretations of the natural world against his own experience of it. In 1802 he exhibited at the Academy for the first time and also received an invitation to become a drawing master at a military establishment. This he rejected, having now set himself a more ambitious goal. Constable returned one day from Beaumont's collection 'with a deep conviction', he told Dunthorne, 'of the truth of Sir Joshua Reynolds's observation that "there is no *easy* way of becoming a good painter". It can only be obtained by long contemplation and incessant labour in the executive part . . . I shall shortly return to Bergholt where I shall make some laborious studies from nature – and I shall endeavour to get a pure and unaffected representation of the scenes that may employ me'. He continued to make outdoor oil studies until the 1820s. Tentative at first, and carrying overtones of Claude and Gainsborough, his sketching had become by about 1810 a fluent and distinctly personal means of getting at his material, as can be seen from such examples in the Gallery as 'A Lane near Flatford(?)' and 'Dedham from near Gun Hill, Langham'. His great friend Archdeacon John Fisher found a parallel in Gilbert White's method of 'narrowly observing & noting down all the natural occurrances that came within his view', but the entries on natural phenomena in Coleridge's notebooks are perhaps still closer to the spirit of Constable's observations. The end to which his studies (in pencil as well as oil) were directed was the production of paintings for exhibition and, Constable hoped, for sale. The connection between the two types of work was, however, rarely simple. Many of Constable's compositions had their beginning in studies made years before, which he took up and further modified in studio sketches before proceeding to the final canvas. The Tate Gallery's 'Glebe Farm' paintings of about 1830, for example, derive from an oil sketch made around 1810–15, while 'The Valley Farm' of 1835 can be traced back through various intermediary stages to a drawing of about 1812.

In his exhibition pieces Constable tried to synthesise the particular knowledge gained through his outdoor sketches and to realise those larger images of his native countryside which had preoccupied him, he said, even before he became a painter. Unfortunately, few others understood or appreciated what he was up to. His first

John Constable
**Scene on a navigable river
('Flatford Mill')** 1817
Oil on canvas, 40 × 50 (101.7 × 127)

After the deaths of his parents in 1815 and 1816 and his own marriage in the latter year, Constable became an infrequent visitor to his native Suffolk. Affection for the scenes of his childhood became, however, an even stronger driving force in his art and it may not be coincidence that 'Flatford Mill', his first large painting depicting the working life of the Stour, was made at this critical juncture in his career. Following it, Constable embarked on his great series of six-foot canvases of the river and its human activity: 'The White Horse', 'Stratford Mill', 'The Hay Wain', and so on. 'I associate my "careless boyhood" to all that

lies on the banks of the *Stour*', he wrote in 1821, 'They made me a painter (& I am gratefull) that is I had often thought of pictures of them before I ever touched a pencil'. The prominent signature on 'Flatford Mill', painted as though scored in the earth by the artist, underlines Constable's close identification with this particular scene of his childhood, the stretch of the river from his father's mill (and the family's residence until 1774) to the footbridge at Flatford. The compositional – and perhaps emotional – pivot of the whole work is a boy astride a towing horse, who waits for a rope to be disconnected before riding to the other side of the bridge, where the barges will be picked up again after being poled under it. In the six-foot canvases which followed, Constable was able to resolve some

of the difficulties he encountered in putting together the 1817 painting. The compositional devices here are a little too apparent. The boy and his horse do not really stand up to the barrage of tree shadows, *repoussoir* elements (the mooring post and the hat in the foreground), barge poles and other woodwork that direct our attention to them. In detail, however, the picture contains some of Constable's loveliest passages: the man with his scythe in the field at the right, for example, or the area around the lock. Whatever its awkwardnesses, the picture epitomises a period in Constable's life when he still found it possible, even necessary, to create images of man and nature at peace with each other. Under summer skies, the pace is leisurely; as yet there are no thunder clouds on the horizon.

John Constable, **Hampstead Heath with the House called 'The Salt Box'** *c.*1820

John Constable, **Admiral's House, Hampstead** *c.*1820–5

John Constable, **Chain Pier, Brighton** exhibited 1827

major Suffolk landscape, 'Dedham Vale: Morning', was shown at the Academy in 1811 but passed unnoticed. His first sale to a stranger came only in 1814, when the bookseller James Carpenter gave him twenty guineas and some books for his previous year's production. To professional worries were added the frustrations of his long drawn-out engagement to Maria Bicknell, whose family opposed their marriage.

Finding only occasional buyers for his landscapes, Constable was forced to supplement the allowance he received from his parents by undertaking portrait commissions and other 'jobs'. One of his earliest and largest efforts of this kind was the group portrait of the Bridges family, painted in 1804, while his later portraiture is represented in the Tate by pictures of Dr and Mrs Andrews. Faced with more sympathetic sitters, Constable revealed considerable potential in this field, as his portrait of Maria Bicknell shows. This was painted in 1816, a few months before they married. With a new confidence (and soon to be relieved of some of his financial worries), Constable set his sights even higher. Although 'Flatford Mill', exhibited in 1817, remained on his hands, he began the first of his six-foot canvases of river subjects, 'The White Horse', showing it at the Academy in 1819. This time his work was, his biographer C.R. Leslie remarked, 'too large to remain unnoticed'. Constable was finally elected an A.R.A. later that year, at

the age of forty-three. Fisher bought both this painting and its successor, 'Stratford Mill'. The next two pictures in the series, 'The Hay Wain' and 'View on the Stour near Dedham' went to the Parisian dealer Arrowsmith in 1824 and created a lively, if short-lived, interest in France.

In the construction of these large compositions Constable found the need of some intermediate stage between his small oil studies and the final canvases. Working on a canvas the same size as the final one, he tried to correlate the mass of diverse material that he wanted to utilise. The last work for which he painted one of these full-size, trial sketches appears to have been 'Hadleigh Castle', shown in 1829; the sketch is in the Tate.

Although Constable never lost his affection for the scenery of the Suffolk–Essex border, he gradually extended the range of his subject matter. His visits, in particular, to Salisbury, where his friend Fisher lived, and to Brighton, where he took Maria for the sake of her health, provided him with much new material. But it was Hampstead that became the main focus of his later work. The Constables first took a house there, in addition to their London home, in 1819; thereafter they rented a house at Hampstead for part of each year, except 1824, finally acquiring a more permanent home there in 1827. In his painting Constable familiarised himself with Hampstead Heath by making innumerable studies of the same scenes under different conditions. The views westward from the heath, looking towards Harrow, for example, were tried again and again, in much the same way that in earlier years he had repeatedly studied the view from Langham, looking down to Dedham and the Stour estuary. But at Hampstead Constable became more acutely conscious of weather as a continuous phenomenon, for ever altering the appearance of the landscape: he became, indeed, more aware of the change-fulness of nature as a whole. In 1821 and 1822 he undertook an intense study of the most transient of all natural phenomena, the sky, producing dozens of cloud sketches, annotating them with precise details of time, wind direction and so on. In his larger paintings of the late 1820s and 1830s placid summer scenes gave way to more unsettled conditions: a choppy sea and figures scurrying before the wind in 'Chain Pier, Brighton'; the first glints of sunrise after a stormy night in 'Hadleigh Castle'; and in 'Salisbury Cathedral, from the Meadows', for which the Tate has a small sketch, the cathedral rising defiantly through thunder clouds while a rainbow arches overhead. Constable increasingly identified his own states of mind with these restless phenomena. When Maria died of tuberculosis in 1828 he felt that 'the face of the World is totally changed to me'. The following year, at the age of fifty-two, Constable was at last elected to full membership of the Royal Academy, only to be told by its President that he was 'peculiarly fortunate' to be chosen when there were History Painters on the list. In an attempt to counter the neglect and misunderstanding of his art he collaborated with David Lucas on a series of mezzotints after his works, accompanied by explanatory texts. Meeting failure even here, Constable wrote to Leslie: 'every gleam of sunshine is blighted to me in the art at least. Can it therefore be wondered at that I paint continual storms?'.

John Constable, **The Valley Farm** 1835

John Constable, **Sketch for 'Hadleigh Castle'** c.1828–9

Landscape Painting
1800–1850

During the first half of the nineteenth century landscape painting became for many British artists, and for a sizeable part of the picture-buying public, the most important branch of art. Even the Royal Academy lecturers, who had regarded landscape as a very poor relation of History Painting, came grudgingly to acknowledge its new status. But while the genre developed and expanded, its growth was by no means straightforward; many landscapists found themselves left out on a limb.

A good deal was already happening at the very beginning of the century. One of the more interesting features of the first decade is an apparent increase in the practice of outdoor oil-sketching: Constable's and Turner's studies are not isolated instances of this activity. John Varley's pupils, for example, were encouraged to 'Go to Nature for everything'. In 1806 two of them, John Linnell and William Henry Hunt, were sent out from Varley's summer house at Twickenham to 'make such transcripts as they could' in the locality. To Varley, another of whose dicta was 'Nature wants cooking', Linnell's and Hunt's oil studies of bits of broken river bank, sections of tree trunk and fragments of old cottages, may well have seemed somewhat raw. Comparable oil studies by Mulready, Delamotte and others are known. With the exception of Linnell, however, none of these

artists managed to make such outdoor work the basis of a career in landscape painting. Even if the knowledge gleaned from close observation of natural phenomena could be used in the creation of larger paintings, there was little public interest in the end product. Mulready's early efforts in landscape came to an end in 1812 when two canvases of this sort were rejected as too literal by the person who had commissioned them; he is said to have refused to 'recognise them as pictures'. Thereafter Mulready concentrated on genre painting, which had already entered incidentally into such works as 'Cottage and Figures' of 1807. Linnell encountered similar difficulties when he tried to sell his 'Kensington Gravel Pits' in 1813 but he was able to sustain his own brand of 'naturalism' for a number of years and to instil some of it into the work of his future son-in-law, Samuel Palmer.

John Crome, **The Poringland Oak** c.1818–20

Another artist who may have benefited from Linnell's example was George Robert Lewis, with whom he toured Wales in 1813. Lewis was, it seems, only briefly a landscape painter but his 'Harvest Scene' of 1815 (described as 'Painted on the Spot' when exhibited the following year) is one of the most memorable images of the whole period.

Another feature of the first years of the nineteenth century was the formation of artists' associations and exhibiting societies which had a distinct bias towards

George Robert Lewis, **Hereford, Dynedor and the Malvern Hills, from the Haywood Lodge, Harvest Scene, Afternoon** 1815

John Linnell
Kensington Gravel Pits 1813
Oil on canvas,
28 × 42 (71.1 × 106.7)

The gravel pits at Kensington were situated on both sides of the road now called Notting Hill Gate; the village at this point was also known as Kensington Gravel Pits. Linnell and Mulready lived there from 1809 to 1811 and some of their best work resulted from studies made in the area. Another artist who worked there was William Henry Hunt. A record survives of how Linnell and Hunt would go 'to Kensington Gravel Pits, then open country, and sitting down before any common object, the paling of a cottage garden, a mossy wall, or an old post, try to imitate it minutely'. Careful observation of common objects and, in the case of Linnell's gravel pit picture, common people was not what the picture-buying public wanted, however. Linnell painted 'Kensington Gravel Pits' in 1811–12

and exhibited it at the British Institution in 1813. Flaxman admired it but no trace remains of any other positive response on that occasion. Linnell was angry that the Institution itself did not step in to buy the work: 'This the painter always considered', wrote his first biographer, 'a proof of the apathy and neglect which characterized the doings of the Institution, which was supported by wealthy patrons whose object was the encouragement of this description of art'. At the Liverpool Academy later that year the painting was bought for forty-five guineas by Thomas Bewick's pupil Henry Hole, whose training may be supposed to have given him a more than usual sympathy for the sort of detailed observation, and even the sort of subject matter, of Linnell's picture.

John Sell Cotman, **The Drop Gate** *c.*1826

landscape painting. In London the Society of Painters in Water-Colours and the British Institution, founded in 1804 and 1805 respectively, were much more orientated than the Royal Academy towards this branch of art. A visitor to the first exhibition in 1808 of a further institution, the Associated Artists in Watercolours, was struck by 'the overwhelming proportion of landscapes, a proportion almost as unreasonable as that of the portraits at Somerset House', that is, the Royal Academy. Outside London, the Norwich Society was founded in 1803 by John Crome and others. On the whole a conservative body, its roots led either directly or through Gainsborough to seventeenth-century Dutch landscape painting, which was well represented at the time in local collections. Crome himself painted mainly Norfolk scenes and was particularly attracted to the barren heaths of the county and to its woods and river estuaries. The other leading member of the Society, John Sell Cotman, produced much of his best work outside East Anglia; his keen sense of pattern is also untypical of the other members. Despite the existence of its Society, Norwich was not an easy market for artists. Both Crome and Cotman depended largely on teaching for their living and Cotman had also to work for many years on topographical and antiquarian publications.

On the other side of the country, an informal sketching club was formed in Bristol in the early years of the century and by 1820 the Irish-born artist Francis Danby had joined its ranks. Danby painted a number of small, detailed landscapes of the area which are very distinctive: intimate pictures in which Bristolians are shown enjoying their local scenery. In the 1820s he also began painting works of a very different sort, aimed at a London rather than a Bristol audience. These were large canvases in the manner of John Martin and it was with one of them, 'The Delivery of Israel out of Egypt' (now at Preston), that in 1825 he scored his first real public success. Martin's and Danby's biblical pictures are as much subject paintings as landscapes and they will be mentioned again in a later section. Half-way between his Bristol landscapes and his biblical subjects were the imaginary landscapes which Danby once called his 'poetical attempts'. Their character is reflected in 'The Tranquil Lake', a painting currently attributed to another Bristol artist, Danby's follower James Johnson.

James Ward, **Lake and Tower in De Tabley Park** 1814

Richard Parkes Bonington, **Near Boulogne** 1823–4

Outside such regional schools as Norwich and Bristol (themselves, as we have seen, by no means homogenous), landscape painters pursued any number of different interests. James Ward spent many of his ninety-odd years painting animals and, taking the place of human figures, they played a special role in his landscapes. Ward said he regarded the foremost bull in 'Tabley Lake and Tower' as 'the Adonis' of his picture; a more massive white bull stands like a sentinel in 'Gordale Scar', painted in 1811–15. These menacing creatures inhabit equally forbidding landscapes. Gordale Scar is inflated to megalomanic proportions, topped off with rolling thunder clouds. In the Tabley picture Ward more modestly attempted the effect of 'a close sultry day, what is vulgarly called a muggy or a murky day' with a thunder storm still only brewing. Linnell, Crome, Ward and others remained firmly wedded, in their different ways, to the British scene. Other artists sought fresh landscape material on the Continent and, later, in the near and middle East. Roberts, Prout, Cotman, Bonington, Callcott, Eastlake, Holland, Lear and J.F. Lewis are only a few of the many who worked extensively abroad. Bonington spent nearly the whole of his short career on the Continent and can be regarded as virtually a French artist. 'Near Boulogne' of 1823–4 is characteristic of his fluent manner, which Constable deplored as assuming 'great dash' to no ends but which Bonington's friend Delacroix greatly admired. The East began to have a strong pull for British landscape and subject painters from the 1830s onwards. The most dedicated visitor to these parts was probably John Frederick Lewis, who lived for ten years in Egypt, having established himself, Thackeray discovered, 'in the most complete Oriental fashion'. His extremely detailed, brilliantly coloured paintings of desert and harem scenes caused a sensation when he returned to London in 1851.

Although a substantial public interest in landscape painting developed during the period under discussion, there were many things the market would not take. Landscapes with no ostensible 'subject', or with one to which only the artist was privy, were rarely in demand. One of Cotman's etchings failed to interest subscribers, the artist was told, 'because it might have been *anywhere*. Two-thirds of mankind, you know, mind more *what* is represented than how it is done.' And landscapes which had 'disagreeable' subjects fared no better. 'Paint something fit to see', was the sermon the Revd John Eagles addressed (in verse) to 'painters of dead stumps, old barges, and canals, and pumps . . .', chief among whom was Constable. Another landscape painter, William Collins, came quickly to realise that 'A painter should choose those subjects with which most people associate pleasant circumstances. It is not sufficient that a scene pleases *him*'. Collins, Creswick and other popular landscapists settled for a combination of landscape (not too

finely observed) and figures (engaged on some harmless anecdotal business). Collins specialised in beach scenes with children, Creswick in woods and streams with adults wandering about. By the middle of the century Linnell too was taking a soft line, fulfilling orders from dealers like Gambart for easily repeated harvest scenes and the like. At about the same time, the advice Linnell had once received from Varley ('Go to Nature for everything') was being offered in a more sophisticated form by Ruskin to a new generation of painters: what sort of nature they, the Pre-Raphaelites, found when they got there will be seen in a later section.

David Cox, **A Windy Day** 1850

William Collins, **Cromer Sands** 1846

Drawings and Watercolours: Eighteenth and Nineteenth Centuries

John Robert Cozens, **Padua** after 1782

There was (and is) no subject which could not be rendered in pencil or wash, pen and ink or watercolour, from preliminary notations of ideas or detailed studies of landscape and figures to fully elaborated compositions. Almost all artists who have painted on canvas have also left evidence of their initial instinct to draw, in line or colour, upon paper, often thereby revealing a spontaneity and expressive power which is partly lost in oils, and invariably adding to our understanding of their work on canvas. After the rich deliberations of Reynolds' various self portraits in oils, for instance, his 'Self Portrait as a Figure of Horror', swiftly executed in chalk, affords a revealing glimpse of this forceful master of the grand manner working urgently upon a comparatively small piece of paper. A pen and ink study of 'Trees and Undergrowth' by Frederick Sandys, to take a very different example, shows a painter best known for his portraits of moody girls biting rose-stalks now concentrating, intent and absorbed, upon the minutiae of landscape.

From the middle of the eighteenth century, a steadily increasing number of British draughtsmen worked in watercolour. Many found the medium so satisfying that (like Girtin, for instance) they rarely if ever painted in oils. The earliest watercolourists had seldom attempted anything more than 'tinted drawings'; and their subject-matter was chiefly topographical – views of towns, picturesque antiquities and country houses. As the eighteenth century advanced, popular demand for engraved views of places both at home and abroad ensured a rising market for the competent topographer; and many of them, like Sandby in the eighteenth century or Lear and Roberts in the nineteenth, were much more than merely competent. Turner, Girtin and Cotman all began their careers as architectural topographers.

Well before the end of the eighteenth century, however, Alexander Cozens and Thomas Gainsborough had shown that landscape drawings need not be tied to the particular to be evocative. Alexander Cozens encouraged his pupils to compose landscapes 'by invention', himself producing highly imaginative pen and wash drawings whose mountains, trees and lakes are drawn from the mind's eye; his work, though low-keyed in colour (indeed, chiefly monochrome) is intense in tone and powerfully charged with an almost surreal feeling for nature. Gainsborough's landscape drawings, also largely monochrome, are generalised in a different way. He arranged and rearranged the familiar ingredients of English landscape to produce a series of perfectly balanced and melodious variations on the theme that 'One part of a picture ought to be like the first part of a Tune, that you could guess what follows, and that makes the second part of the Tune. . .'.

The most profoundly influential watercolourist was the eighteenth century's least assertive personality, Alexander Cozens' son John Robert Cozens. Cozens broke through the earlier tradition of the 'tinted drawing' in which thin washes of local colour were applied over an already distinct monochrome outline; instead, with a minimum of preliminary pencilling, he used watercolour for its own expressive qualities, controlling tones through broken washes and minute brush-strokes or dabs of one colour upon another, and charging his landscapes with drama, atmosphere and poetry in a highly personal manner which owed nothing to the topographical tradition. Cozens' palette was muted, and the prevailing mood in his work is melancholy; by 1794 he was incurably insane. His drawings were collected by some of the most

Thomas Girtin, **The White House, Chelsea** 1800

J.M.W. Turner, **Luxembourg** *c.*1826

David Cox, **Near the Pont d'Arcole, Paris** 1829

discerning patrons of the day, including William Beckford (who owned 'Padua'), Sir George Beaumont and Dr Thomas Monro. Monro established an 'Academy' in his house, inviting younger artists – Turner and Girtin among them – to study by copying the works of Cozens in particular. Cozens' influence can also be seen in the restrained and gravely beautiful watercolours ('Derwentwater' or 'Appleby', for instance) of Monro's friend Thomas Hearne. Constable, whose own draughtsmanship remained a very individual manner of transcribing observations from nature, himself owned at least one of Cozens' watercolours, and acclaimed Cozens as 'the greatest genius that ever touched landscape'.

Turner made his name as a watercolourist, exhibiting nothing in oils before 1796. He was to continue to work in watercolour all his life, surpassing all others in his range of brilliant colour and technical inventiveness, defying imitation. A regularly changing selection of Turner's watercolours is shown at the Tate. The work of Thomas Girtin, Turner's tragically short-lived con-

temporary, was less superficially dazzling but more influential. Girtin's mastery of breadth and deep colour is brilliantly exemplified in 'The White House, Chelsea' and in 'Bamburgh Castle'.

Rowlandson meanwhile pursued an independent course; flexing the old tradition of first drawing, then colouring, he produced a prodigious series of distinctive designs, energetically cursive in line and delicate in colouring, in which boisterous incident by no means excludes a charming rococo delineation of landscape (as in 'Landscape, Isle of Wight'). In the same tradition William Blake pursued his own highly personal course. More in the mainstream of the maturing British watercolour tradition, yet still very personal, are Cornelius Varley's atmospheric landscapes, delicate but never insubstantial, and Joshua Cristall's watercolours, more earthbound but still imaginative, whether he is dreaming of Arcady or recording observations on Hastings beach.

With John Sell Cotman we encounter an artist who, while learning from both Cozens and Girtin, displayed a highly original talent, hardly applauded in his lifetime, perhaps because his work often seems a century ahead of its time in its flat angular patterns and vivid colour juxtapositions. The controlled force of Cotman's draughtsmanship is manifest in such drawings as 'The Ramparts, Domfront' and the deceptively simple pen and wash 'Durham'. David Cox's work is distinguished by robust vigour, whether he depicts 'Still Life' (kitchen vessels on a ledge) or the bustling life 'Near the Pont d'Arcole, Paris'. Some of Peter de Wint's harvesting scenes capture a sense of hard work on hot days, but perhaps his chief success is with the broad panoramic view, barely peopled, richly and harmoniously coloured.

Clearly there is as much scope for idiosyncrasy in drawings and watercolours as in oil paintings, if not more. The idiosyncratic certainly includes Samuel Palmer's visionary art and the hallucinatory work of Richard Dadd. In Edward Lear's quirky line and brilliant colouring (as in 'Philates') there are odd echoes of the equally idiosyncratic earlier work of Francis Towne. There has always been scope, too, for technical experiment. The Pre-Raphaelites, for instance, brought to watercolour the same intensity that they brought to oils, virtually excluding that translucency which, it might be argued, is watercolour's supreme advantage over oils.

Subject Painting 1800–1860

While the notion of High Art or History Painting still preoccupied art theorists in the early nineteenth century, there was a growing recognition that this kind of painting had in practice failed. 'Our age, when compared with former ages', Fuseli told the Royal Academy students in 1825, 'has but little occasion for great works, and that is the reason why so few are produced: – the ambition, activity, and spirit of public life is shrunk to the minute detail of domestic arrangements – every thing that surrounds us tends to show us in private, is become snug, less, narrow, pretty, insignificant . . .'. Thackeray, twenty years later, was very willing to settle for this state of affairs. An unassuming little domestic piece was 'the sort of picture that is good to paint nowadays – kindly, beautiful, inspiring delicate sympathies, and awakening tender good-humour'. According to the self-appointed guardian of High Art, B.R.Haydon, the rot had started with David Wilkie, who 'by his talent has done great injury to the taste of the Nation. Nothing bold or masculine or grand or powerful touches an English Connoiseur – it must be small and highly wrought, and vulgar & humorous & broad & palpable. I question whether Reynolds would now make the impression he did, so completely is the taste ebbing to a Dutch one'.

Wilkie had set the scene with his Teniers-like 'Village Politicians', shown in 1806, and 'The Blind Fiddler' in

Sir David Wilkie, **The Blind Fiddler** 1806

1807, the former purchased by Lord Mansfield and the latter commissioned by Sir George Beaumont. A new generation of middle-class collectors was soon to follow this aristocratic lead; through engravings an even wider audience was reached. An instant success, Wilkie quickly had imitators. William Mulready entered the field in 1808 with 'The Rattle', and William Collins and others followed. Even Haydon was forced to lower his sights occasionally and paint humorous subjects, though in a Hogarthian manner rather than in Wilkie's 'highly wrought' style. After several years spent on the Continent in the 1820s, Wilkie himself began to paint in a different way. His later works owed more to Rembrandt and the Spanish masters than to Teniers and Ostade, and

William Mulready, **The Last In** 1835

his subject matter also became more dramatic. Wilkie helped to create a fashion among younger artists for Spanish subjects. Following in his footsteps, if not in his style, both J.F. Lewis and John Phillip earned the sobriquet 'Spanish' for their work in the Peninsula. While Wilkie's pictures became darker in tone, Mulready developed a high colour key which became a model for the Pre-Raphaelites. Humorous scenes, usually involving children, remained, however, his favourite subjects. Thomas Webster shared this predilection, making a speciality of schoolroom antics.

Animals proved equally amenable to anecdotal treatment, for example by J.F. Herring in 'The Frugal Meal' (horses), George Lance in 'The Red Cap' (a monkey) and Edwin Landseer in 'Dignity and Impudence' (dogs). Title alone was certainly no guide to subject matter – later in the century T.S. Cooper exhibited a cattle picture called 'Separated, but not Divorced'. It was Landseer who dominated this area of the market, with his canine conversation pieces, 'monkeyana' and episodes in the lives and deaths of Highland stags. 'The creatures of his

Sir Edwin Landseer, **Dignity and Impudence** 1839

pencil', wrote a contributor to *The Art-Union* in 1848, 'seem to possess minds and passions scarcely inferior to our own.' Landseer achieved a huge popular success and a vast fortune, the latter chiefly through copyright sales to print-publishers. He was Queen Victoria's favourite artist and, like Wilkie before him, received a knighthood and came near to being elected President of the Royal Academy.

While many painters of genre invented their own subjects, others turned to literature for theirs. Innumerable scenes from *The Vicar of Wakefield, Gil Blas, Don Quixote, Tristram Shandy,* and so on, appeared at the Academy and quickly reappeared in the collections of such men as John Sheepshanks (son of a wealthy Leeds clothier) and Robert Vernon (horse-dealer extraordinary), both of whom left their pictures to the nation. Picturesque incidents from English history were also very popular. Leslie, Newton, E.M. Ward and, in their early work, Egg and Frith, were among the artists who specialised in these lines.

Not all subject painters dealt in anecdotal material. Although History Painting as practised by Haydon was little in demand, there were markets for exotic or sensational treatments of the sort of subjects traditionally associated with it. William Etty's voluptuous mythologies went down well with the new collectors (Gillot, the Birmingham pen manufacturer, for example, was a valuable patron), whether or not they achieved the artist's aim 'to paint some great moral on the heart'. John Martin's biblical spectaculars – fantastic landscape or architectural sets peopled with myriads of diminutive,

gesturing figures – had a wide audience, many of the paintings being extensively toured as well as engraved by the artist. His last major works, the three large 'Judgement' pictures of the early 1850s, were still touring the country twenty years later. After a period of landscape painting in Bristol, Francis Danby began exhibiting Martinesque pictures in London in the 1820s but a personal scandal forced him to flee the country in 1829. The gigantic 'Deluge' of 1840 was intended to re-establish his reputation on his return to England. Supernatural happenings of a different order were the concern of Richard Dadd, Robert Huskisson, J.A. Fitzgerald and other painters of 'fairy' subjects. Dadd's 'The Fairy Feller's Master-Stroke' is the best known example of the genre, though Dadd, incarcerated in criminal lunatic asylums for forty-two years of his life, ranged over much else besides.

William Etty, **Candaules, King of Lydia, shews his Wife by Stealth to Gyges** exhibited 1830

John Martin, **The Great Day of His Wrath** 1851–3

Richard Dadd,
The Fairy Feller's Master-Stroke 1855–64

Around the middle of the century, scenes from contemporary life re-entered the repertoire of subject painting. The artist who did most to promote this sort of picture was William Powell Frith, whose first major essay in the genre, 'Ramsgate Sands', was bought by Queen Victoria. 'The Derby Day', 'The Railway Station' and other panoramas of modern life followed. They proved extremely popular and very profitable, the engraving and exhibition rights being at least as valuable as the paintings themselves. These works and such smaller modern life pictures as Egley's 'Omnibus Life' and Houghton's 'Ramsgate Sands' are just as anecdotal in character as Wilkie's productions at the beginning of the century. Some artists tried to add weight to their depiction of the contemporary scene by choosing less entertaining subjects. In the 1840s Richard Redgrave painted several pictures showing the misfortunes of young working women, especially seamstresses and governesses, while G.F. Watts painted a female suicide washed-up under Waterloo Bridge. It was, however, the Pre-Raphaelites who really established this kind of modern morality picture in the 1850s. Under their influence, Augustus Egg turned from costume pieces to tell the tragedy of a broken family in 'Past and Present', the young Calderon scored his first success with 'Broken Vows' and an otherwise unmemorable art teacher, H.A. Bowler, posed the question: 'Can these dry bones live?'.

Augustus Leopold Egg, **Past and Present, No. 1** 1858

William Powell Frith
The Derby Day 1858
Oil on canvas,
40 × 88 (101.6 × 223.5)

Following the success of 'Ramsgate Sands', bought by the Queen in 1854, Frith set about looking for another subject which would give him, he later recalled, 'the opportunity of showing an appreciation of the infinite variety of everyday life'. The idea of a race-course setting came to him in 1854 but it was not until his first visit to Epsom two years later that he began to plan the picture. After 'fifteen months incessant labour' Frith completed 'The Derby Day' and exhibited it at the Royal Academy in 1858. The painting had been commissioned by Jacob Bell, founder of the Pharmaceutical Society, after seeing Frith's preliminary oil sketch in 1856. Bell had many contacts in the art world and was assiduous in finding models for the picture: Frith recorded that he owed 'every female figure . . . except two or three, to the foraging of my employer'. A fellow artist, J.F. Herring senior, supplied a drawing of race-horses for Frith to use and Frith also commissioned Robert Howlett to take photographs of the Epsom scene for him. At the Academy 'The Derby Day' created

such a sensation that Bell demanded a rail to protect it from the crowds, the first time this had been necessary since Wilkie exhibited his 'Chelsea Pensioners' in 1822. At the close of the exhibition Frith's picture went on a world tour arranged by the dealer Gambart, who owned the engraving and exhibition rights in the work. Although one of the most popular paintings of the nineteenth century, 'The Derby Day' was given a mixed reception by other artists and by critics. Ruskin decided that it was 'quite proper and desirable that this English carnival should be painted; and of the entirely popular manner of painting, which, however, we must remember, is necessarily, because popular, stooping and restricted, I have never seen an abler example. The drawing of the distant figures seems to me especially dexterous and admirable; but it is very difficult to characterize the picture in accurate general terms. It is a kind of cross between John Leech and Wilkie, with a dash of daguerreotype here and there, and some pretty seasoning with Dickens's sentiment.'

The Pre-Raphaelite Brotherhood and its Followers

The Pre-Raphaelite Brotherhood – the 'P.R.B.' – was formed in 1848 by seven young men, notably Holman Hunt, Millais and Rossetti. Mostly students at the Royal Academy, they were dissatisfied with the state of art in England as displayed in the teaching and exhibitions of the Academy because it seemed to lack vigour, seriousness and sincerity. They believed these qualities had flourished in Italy and northern Europe before the time of Raphael; in this 'primitive' art they felt a strength which they attributed to its sincerity of purpose and, especially, the close observation and depiction of nature. In contrast, contemporary art seemed feeble because it ignored nature and relied too heavily on academic conventions. Unlike the German 'Nazarene' painters earlier in the century the P.R.B. did not want to revive archaic styles of painting as such; they chose instead to follow the advice of the art critic John Ruskin to 'go to nature', and, in their own words, to aim at 'serious and elevated intention of a subject, along with earnest scrutiny of visible facts, and an earnest endeavour to present them veraciously and exactly'. Strict adherence to these principles is evident in several early P.R.B. works such as Millais' 'Christ in the House of His Parents' and Hunt's 'Claudio and Isabella', with their profoundly serious subjects, careful rendering of light and texture, high-key colouring (which was achieved by painting over a white ground as early Italian fresco and tempera painters had done), and 'earnest scrutiny' of natural appearances down to the minutest detail. Millais, for example, found a carpenter's shop in Oxford Street for his setting, and employed a carpenter as a model so he could depict the correct musculature of Joseph's arm.

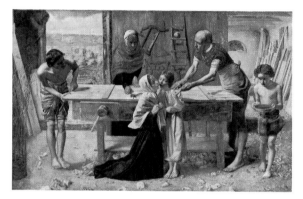

Sir John Everett Millais, **Christ in the House of His Parents (The Carpenter's Shop)** 1849–50

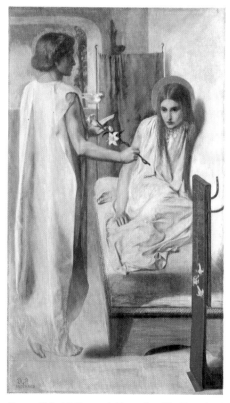

Dante Gabriel Rossetti, **Ecce Ancilla Domini!** (**'The Annunciation'**) 1849–50

Even Rossetti, the most extraordinary personality in the P.R.B. and the least trained of the three leaders, attempted detailed historical veracity in his Annunciation scene, although the picture is testimony not so much to P.R.B. ideas as to the curious quality of his powerful imagination. It is highly personal, unlike any other depiction of that often painted subject, and, in common with many of his paintings, intimately concerned with his work as a poet. Millais' picture received the most adverse criticism in the press; it was principally his choice of a sacred subject and his grimly realistic treatment of it that horrified the critics, particularly Charles Dickens, who called the painting 'mean, odious, repulsive and revolting'. It seemed sacrilegious, for example, to represent Joseph with gnarled workman's hands and dirty fingernails. Hunt, with his remarkable powers of observation and painstaking execution, went on to use his art to moralise on the spiritual ills of contemporary society. From 'Claudio and Isabella', a scene from Shakespeare's *Measure for Measure* illustrating a moral dilemma (should

William Holman Hunt, **Claudio and Isabella** 1850

Isabella surrender her virginity in return for her brother Claudio's life?), Hunt turned to the morality of modern life with 'The Awakening Conscience', which was intended, in the words of the artist, 'to show how the still small voice speaks to a soul in the turmoil of life'. The picture is full of symbols which serve to orchestrate the main theme, that of a 'fallen' woman whose conscience is suddenly awakened to the innocence of her past and the present error of her ways. Having finished this painting, Hunt departed for the Middle East, as he believed he could only paint Biblical subjects in the Bible lands. Hunt remained faithful to Pre-Raphaelite principles for the rest of his long life, but, ironically, it was his departure that marked the end of the P.R.B. Rossetti, whose powerful personality seems to have been the driving force behind the P.R.B., had already transferred his interest to the beautiful young girl who was to become his model, Elizabeth Siddal.

Of the other founder members of the P.R.B. little need be said. Thomas Woolner, a sculptor, emigrated to Australia for a few years, and after his return made a respectably successful career as a portrait sculptor. Rossetti's brother William Michael does not seem to have painted at all, and became an art critic and historian of Pre-Raphaelitism. Frederic George Stephens also became a professional art critic, but painted a few pictures

in the early 1850s of which the curious 'Mother and Child' is the most accomplished. James Collinson, for a short while engaged to be married to Christina Rossetti, left the P.R.B. in 1850 because of his Roman Catholic beliefs, and subsequently entered a monastery for a few years. On his return he resumed painting, his most

William Holman Hunt, **The Awakening Conscience** 1853–7

Ford Madox Brown, **The Last of England** 1864–6

famous picture being 'The Empty Purse', of which there are several versions, one in the Tate Gallery.

However, the Pre-Raphaelite circle was by this time wider than the P.R.B., and from the beginning had included Ford Madox Brown, a few years older than the others, who influenced the younger artists and was in turn influenced by them, particularly by their intense observation of nature. Like Hunt, he became concerned with serious moral subjects, and with criticism of modern society, but his approach was less allegorical and more direct than Hunt's, as in 'The Last of England', which records the unhappy plight of those such as Woolner, forced to emigrate because of lack of employment at home.

With the doctrine of 'truth to nature' behind their work, the Pre-Raphaelites of course were much concerned with landscape painting, not only as backgrounds for narrative pictures, but as a subject in its own right. At Hendon in the summer of 1855, Ford Madox Brown painted 'The Hayfield', which recorded the strange

William Dyce, **Pegwell Bay, Kent – a Recollection of October 5th 1858** 1859–60

Ford Madox Brown, **The Hayfield** 1855–6

William Holman Hunt, **Our English Coasts, 1852** (**'Strayed Sheep'**) 1852

effects of light on colours and of the interaction of colours in the devoted manner that the Impressionists later adopted. Brown wrote about this picture that in the glow of early twilight the hay had seemed to be red or pink in contrast to the green grass. The painter himself rests in the foreground, with his paint-box, palette, camp-stool and umbrella; Brown, like Millais, discovered the hazards of painting out the doors and described the weather while he worked on this picture as 'most trying'. By contrast, Hunt's painting of sheep straying on a cliff-top echoes contemporary fears of anarchy at home and invasion from abroad, though this is only hinted at in the title Hunt gave the work when it was first exhibited – 'Our English Coasts, 1852'. Ruskin valued it more for its absolutely faithful depiction of sunlight. The strangest of all Pre-Raphaelite landscapes must be William Dyce's 'Pegwell Bay', and the mystery begins with the title, which continues 'A Recollection of October 5th, 1858'. It was on 5 October that Donati's comet was spectacularly visible in England and Dyce depicts it in the sky. Dyce closely followed Ruskin's advice to go to nature, rejecting nothing and selecting nothing; his picture leaves no stone unpainted. Part of the strangeness of the picture's atmosphere is due to the pallid autumn light and the time of day, just before evening when the beach would have been deserted. But the figures are deliberately placed apart, each unaware of the others' presence, and none of them is looking at the comet in the sky. They seem to inhabit a world of dreams such as Salvador Dali might have imagined. Perhaps too, the picture illustrates Ruskin's idea that 'beauty is continually mingled with the shadow of death'.

Millais' career took a different course from Hunt's moralising brand of Pre-Raphaelitism, and ended far away from Pre-Raphaelitism altogether. Following the scathing criticism of his early works, he turned to less controversial and more sentimental subjects such as

Sir John Everett Millais
Ophelia 1852
Oil on canvas,
30 × 44 (76 × 112)

Millais was still in his early twenties when he painted this masterpiece of Pre-Raphaelite art and one of the most striking and haunting images in the history of British painting. It illustrates Queen Gertrude's description in *Hamlet* (Act 4 Scene 7) of Ophelia's suicide: 'There is a willow grows aslant a brook . . . there with fantastic garlands did she come . . . when down her weedy trophies and herself fell in the weeping brook. Her clothes spread wide; and mermaid-like, a-while they bore her up: which time she chanted snatches of old tunes . . .'. In true Pre-Raphaelite fashion, the background was carefully painted from nature, mainly on the banks of the River Ewell near Kingston-on-Thames, during the summer of 1851. Millais recorded that he and Hunt would rise at six, be working by eight, not returning home until seven in the evening, and that he painted sitting by the stream 'tailor-fashion under an umbrella . . . in danger of being blown by the wind into the water'. In the winter he painted in the figure at his London studio, from the model Elizabeth Siddal, who had to lie in a bath of water which the artist tried, unsuccessfully, to keep warm by placing lamps underneath. Despite being painted separately, the landscape and the figure perfectly fuse to convey Ophelia's deadly consummation with the element. Millais not only brilliantly recorded his acute observation of nature, every detail of the flowers and foliage being carefully described, but also achieved a pose and facial expression for Ophelia herself – neither fully conscious nor yet dead – that contribute most to the picture's strange and lasting power. The painting was much admired by John Ruskin, who called it 'the loveliest English landscape, haunted by sorrow'.

Sir John Everett Millais,
The Order of Release 1746 1852–3

'The Order of Release', which although painted in a meticulous Pre-Raphaelite manner, particularly in the brilliant rendering of surface texture, has no detailed background. The plain dark background not only meant that Millais saved a good deal of time, but also that the figures are dramatically spotlit, concentrating our attention on the loyal wife (for whom the model was Ruskin's wife Effie, later to marry Millais) who has secured her husband's release from prison after the Jacobite Rebellion of 1745. This stirring historical narrative, guaranteed to appeal to Victorian taste, achieved great popular and critical acclaim, and Millais went on to enjoy a highly successful career.

Meanwhile, in the 1850s and 1860s, a number of young artists, attracted by the ideals of Pre-Raphaelite painting and encouraged by John Ruskin's writings, particularly his support of the P.R.B., adopted the new principles of conscientiously observed detail, bright colours and intensely emotional subject-matter. One of the earliest and most loyal followers was Arthur Hughes, whose 'April Love' is one of the most beautiful of all Pre-Raphaelite paintings. He shows himself in this picture to be as good a technician as Hunt or Millais, in the painting

of the gauze shawl for example. Hughes specialised in scenes of love, probably inspired by Millais' success with paintings of lovers meeting or parting, such as 'The Order of Release'. But Hughes' pictures are usually imbued with a greater degree of romantic melancholy, as if any rendezvous or tryst were doomed to disappointment; the girl in 'April Love' looks away from the man who is kissing her hand, while a tear trickles down her cheek. It is typical, not only of a Pre-Raphaelite, but of many Victorian artists, to suggest rather than fully explain the narrative of the picture: they sometimes preferred to encourage the viewer to use his own imagination to fill in the details of the stories. This deliberate obscurity, together with the highly emotional character of much Victorian painting, reminds us of its place in the European Romantic movement, as well as its part in Victorian culture.

The closest friend of the P.R.B. was Walter Howell Deverell. He was even proposed, though not elected, a member of the Brotherhood after the resignation of Collinson in 1850, and his painting of 'A Pet', exhibited in 1853, is highly Pre-Raphaelite in technique and mood.

Arthur Hughes, **April Love** 1855–6

Henry Wallis, **Chatterton** 1856

His illness prevented him from achieving much, and he died in 1854 at the age of twenty-six. William Windus was one of the staunchest followers of the Pre-Raphaelites, dealing both with historical and with modern life subjects. His 'Too Late' shares the same intensely sorrowful mood as Hughes' paintings of disappointed love. The young man has returned to find that the girl, presumably his fiancée, has consumption, a common nineteenth-century affliction. The picture is more melodramatic than most Pre-Raphaelite paintings, particularly in the man's theatrical gesture of despair, but, like so many Pre-Raphaelite works, succeeds in conveying genuinely felt emotion by the combination of close attention to detail and intensity of mood, both in the figures and the landscape. One of the most famous historical pictures in the Pre-Raphaelite style is 'Chatterton' painted by Henry Wallis, an artist about whom little is known. Chatterton, a young poet and forger of the 'medieval' Rowley poems, had committed suicide in 1770 at the age of seventeen and was later elevated to the status of a tragic hero by the Romantics. Wallis – in true Pre-Raphaelite fashion – painted the background of his picture from the attic room where Chatterton died, but the direct emotional impact of his scene is achieved more by the harsh lighting, vibrant colours, the Christ-like pose of the dead poet, particularly the eloquence of the lifeless arm and hand, and details such as the phial of poison and torn sheets of poetry on the floor.

There were also artists in the 1850s and 1860s who adapted the meticulously detailed style of the Pre-Raphaelites to their own ends. Martineau's 'The Last Day in the Old Home' is a Hogarthian subject – a moral tale of a dissolute husband who has been reduced to selling his family home and its contents. Egg's three paintings now known as 'Past and Present' deal with the story of an unfaithful wife; the first picture is as painfully detailed and symbolic as Hunt's 'Awakening Conscience'. The 'plots' of paintings like these are very similar to those of the many Victorian novels which dealt with

misfortune and loyalty, profligacy and retribution.

It is ironic that the greatest challenge to the ideals of the Pre-Raphaelites in the 1860s was supported, and in some ways created, by one of the original members of the P.R.B., Rossetti. During the 1850s he had become more and more absorbed in the medieval world and its romance, a world largely of his own imagining, but inspired by his reading of Dante and Malory. He was also obsessed both aesthetically and emotionally by his female sitters, and

William Lindsay Windus, **Too Late** 1858

his later pictures, whatever their ostensible subjects, are really hymns of adoration to the physical beauty of his models. In 'Proserpine' for example, Rossetti invests Jane, William Morris' wife, with an aura of sensuous languor and self-conscious allure. Looking at 'Monna Vanna', it is difficult for us to detect that she is a character from Dante; she is really Rossetti's invention, wearing clothes and jewellery especially designed by Rossetti for his lovely model Alexa Wilding. She, like Proserpine, self-consciously poses for our admiration. This pre-occupation with sheer beauty and mood is very different from the careful and accurate depiction of detail preached and practised by the Pre-Raphaelites. With Whistler and Albert Moore, Rossetti was one of the first nineteenth-century artists to desire and exploit beauty for its own sake, regardless of subject or natural appearances. This desire, when verbalised into a philosophy, principally by

Whistler, was to be the basis of the 'Aesthetic Movement' of the 1880s and 1890s when 'art for art's sake' also resulted in the 'new art' of Europe, the 'Art Nouveau'.

Equally opposed to the 'truth to nature' doctrine of the first Pre-Raphaelites was the younger generation, led by William Morris and Edward Burne-Jones. They were, significantly, disciples of Rossetti, as is evident in their early paintings such as 'Sidonia von Bork' by Burne-Jones and 'Queen Guinevere', Morris' only known oil painting. Morris' work reflects his interest in the middle ages, but, unlike Rossetti, he was not content merely to fantasise in the distant world of Arthurian legend. He saw a practical lesson for modern industrial society in medieval craftsmanship, and went on to become a leading figure in nearly all areas of the decorative arts. He was principally responsible for the 'Arts and Crafts Movement' of the later nineteenth century, which aimed to bring the fine and applied arts together again in an increasingly mechanised world. Although Burne-Jones worked with Morris in many of his schemes, he was primarily a painter, and his philosophy is best defined in his own description of what a painting should be: 'a beautiful romantic dream of something that never was, never will be, . . . in a land no one can define or remember, only desire'.

Dante Gabriel Rossetti, **Proserpine** 1874

William Morris, **Queen Guinevere** 1858

Sir Edward Burne-Jones
**King Cophetua and the Beggar
Maid** 1884
Oil on canvas, $116\frac{1}{2} \times 52\frac{3}{4}$ (265 × 134)

'King Cophetua' has become Burne-Jones' most famous painting, and his wife believed that it showed the distinctive quality of his art more clearly than any other of his works. The story derives from an old legend of a king who found that his love for a beggar maid was greater than his wealth and power. Burne-Jones probably knew the story from Tennyson's treatment of it in his poem *The Beggar Maid*. The artist imagines the king sitting at the maid's feet, his crown in his hands, gazing at her in adoration. He was determined that 'Cophetua should look like a King and the beggar like a Queen', and had certain details such as the crown and the maid's dress specially made for him to paint from. The setting, inspired by fifteenth-century Italian art, particularly Mantegna and Crivelli, is sumptuous and elaborately decorated, enhanced by the highly wrought surface textures and jewel-like colours. The painting, like so much of his work, probably had a deeply personal meaning for Burne-Jones. It is sometimes suggested that the king is the artist himself and the maid his wife. But it is more likely that the maid is Frances Graham, a girl to whom Burne-Jones was devoted. She married in 1883, while the artist was working on the picture, an event which profoundly affected him. It is significant that the maid is holding a bunch of anemones, some of which have fallen on the steps by the king, and indeed the reds and blues of the anemones infuse the whole painting. Anemones are symbolic of rejected love, and it may be that Burne-Jones intended the painting to be an expression of his own feelings at the 'loss' of his beloved Frances. The picture also has another meaning, recognised when it was first exhibited, that of the rejection of worldly wealth and the elevation of love above everything else. This was a message dear to Burne-Jones' heart, and very relevant for late Victorian Britain.

Later Victorian Painting

Frederic, Lord Leighton, **And the Sea gave up the Dead which were in it** exhibited 1892

In the later nineteenth century almost all British painters were conservative in their attitudes, seemingly content to work in the manner approved by the Royal Academy, encouraged by the art critics and admired by an ever-increasing public. The Royal Academy remained in theory the temple of the Grand Manner as created by Reynolds over one hundred years before. Frederic Leighton, for example, impressed the Academy with his medieval and Biblical subjects, and went on in the 1860s to paint classical scenes of considerable grandeur. Although some of his work shares the sensual mood of Rossetti's later paintings, his compositions always have the dignified monumentality thought to be appropriate to Great Art. His 'And the Sea gave up the Dead' represents almost the last phase of the Western artistic tradition, begun in the Renaissance and based on antique example, of belief in the power of the idealised nude or classically draped figure to express the profoundest emotions while participating in an event of the highest importance. The extent of Leighton's success and the

esteem in which he was held may be judged by his election to the Presidency of the Royal Academy and his elevation to the peerage, the only painter ever to be thus honoured.

Even more artistically ambitious was 'England's Michelangelo', George Frederic Watts. He attempted the most solemn subjects, from 'Life's Illusions' of 1849 to 'Love and Life' over thirty years later; both paintings are now in the Tate Gallery, though rarely exhibited, and both are nearly eight feet high. His most famous painting, 'Hope', which has been almost always on public exhibition since Watts himself presented it to the Tate in 1897, reveals an aspect of his work other than the grandeur of Renaissance art, an aspect modern critics have compared with the Symbolism of his contemporaries in France and Belgium. The emotional intensity and self-conscious meaningfulness of 'Hope' certainly go beyond the range of the academic grand manner. Burne-Jones' later work, such as 'King Cophetua and the Beggar Maid' and 'Love and the Pilgrim', also belongs more with European Symbolism. Classicism of a different and less traditional kind may be found in the work of Albert Moore and Alma-Tadema. Far from essaying the great and ennobling stories of classical antiquity, Alma-Tadema depicted everyday life in upper-class ancient Rome, its processions, flirtations, banquets and orgies, always lavish and

George Frederic Watts, **Hope** 1886

Sir John Everett Millais, **The Boyhood of Raleigh** 1870

John William Waterhouse, **The Lady of Shalott** 1888

glamorous in a Hollywood manner. 'A Favourite Custom' – a Royal Academy title intended to delight the spectator who was to find that the picture showed young ladies splashing in a Roman bath – shows his characteristically accomplished sense of design and composition. Other artists who dealt with Greek and Roman subjects in either a grand or an anecdotal way included J.W. Waterhouse in works such as 'Saint Eulalia', but his best-known painting, 'The Lady of Shalott', rather represents the last phase of medievalising Pre-Raphaelitism. Inspired by Rossetti and Burne-Jones, Waterhouse dealt with Tennyson's poem in their intensely Romantic manner. The Lady of Shalott, doomed to live in a tower to weave a tapestry relating the exploits of the Arthurian knights, is forbidden to look from the window. She may see only the reflections in her mirror, in which she sees Sir Lancelot riding by and impulsively turns to look. At once the mirror cracks, the tapestry disintegrates and she accepts her fate – to drift in a boat down the river to her death. Waterhouse depicts this last episode in the story. The Lady sits entranced, surrounded by the remnants of her tapestry, her golden hair and white dress contrasting with the rich greens of the river landscape.

Since the Royal Academy had been founded, artists had depicted scenes from British history. The Victorians, with their love of stirring or affecting anecdote, responded not only to great scenes from the pages of history, but also to the more obscure biographical details of their heroes. One of the most successful and famous of all Victorian pictures was Millais' 'The Boyhood of Raleigh', a 'best seller' as a coloured print and later reproduced in almost every school history book. It appealed on several levels: it is painted in Millais' characteristic later style – rapidly and energetically painted, unlike his early Pre-Raphaelite manner – it presents an affecting image of the young boys listening enthralled to the old sailor's adventures, and it celebrates the triumph of the British Empire, the greatest pride of the later Victorians. Scenes of everyday modern life were also popular, and encompassed comedy and tragedy, high society and the working classes. Upper-class life was not all pleasure, as Orchardson reminded visitors to the Royal Academy every year. Orchardson recorded the little faux-pas that

Sir William Quiller Orchardson, **The First Cloud** 1887

occur at social occasions, but also dealt with more serious subjects such as 'The First Cloud', a 'problem picture' of which the story has to be detected by the spectator. Orchardson's narratives are theatrical tableaux which express the emotions of the actors, in this case the angry exit of a woman at the climax of her first quarrel with her husband. There were also artists in the 1870s and 1880s, notably Holl, Herkomer and Walker, who dealt with serious social problems such as the poverty of the working classes, the danger of their jobs, their lack of jobs, their workhouses and their illnesses. Luke Fildes was

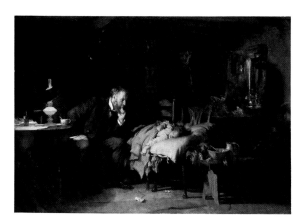

Sir Luke Fildes, **The Doctor** exhibited 1891

one of the foremost painters of this kind, and 'The Doctor' is his most famous painting. The picture needs no explanation, which is probably one of the reasons for its popularity, and the sombre pathos of the spotlit central figure of the dying child is made even more dramatically poignant by the humble setting and the vigil of the anxious doctor, the weeping mother and the stoic figure of the father. The artist's son, who wrote a biography of his father, said that Fildes had been inspired by the memory of the doctor who had tended his first child, who had tragically died while still a baby. The most sophisticated painter of the upper classes and their pleasures was Tissot; his 'Ball on Shipboard' perfectly captures in every detail their appearance and their manners. He shows a sensitive response to colour and particularly the texture and pattern of materials, and his figures never seem to communicate with each other, as if they themselves were only aware of their poses and their clothes. Although painted in a more conventional style, his subjects are similar to those of the French Impressionists, and his sense of design and the apparent informality of his compositions suggest a debt to his friend Degas.

The idea of 'art for art's sake', suggested in many of the paintings of Rossetti and Burne-Jones, was at the foundation of Whistler's mature work. Every aspect of his painting, its subject, meaning, symbolism, its degree of accurate representation, was subordinate to its aesthetic content, its use of line, shape, contour, brushstroke and colouring. 'Nocturne in Blue-Green' is probably the earliest of his series of 'Nocturnes'. It was the art collector Frederick Leyland who suggested this musical term for Whistler's moonlight scenes, and the artist believed it served to 'so poetically say all I want to say and no more than I wish'. He also especially liked the way it irritated the critics. One of the most famous of the series is 'Nocturne in Blue and Gold : Old Battersea Bridge'; it was produced during the famous trial for libel after John Ruskin wrote that Whistler had merely thrown a pot of

paint in the face of the public. The artist won the case but was awarded damages of one farthing, the lowest amount the court could allow. It was the lack of interest in the subject matter, the freedom of the handling of paint, and the lack of 'realistic' description that enraged Ruskin; Whistler's evidently rapid method of painting also conflicted with the Victorian ideal of hard and painstaking work. 'Nocturne in Blue-Green' depicts the view across the Thames from the Battersea side looking towards Chelsea church, but only the outline of the buildings against the sky and the lights from the windows convey the location. The composition is clearly inspired by Japanese art: the high horizon, the surface dominated by the expanse of water and the careful juxtaposition in the foreground of the barge, its lamp and reflection, a standing figure, and Whistler's 'butterfly' signature. Again inspired by Japanese art, Whistler creates a perfect balance between an emphasis on the flat surface of his painting and a sense of distance and depth. But most important to Whistler's art was the concept of colour harmony, a concept expressed in the titles of his pictures. The effect of the cool moonlight on the colour of the river pervades the whole painting, a tonality stressed by the contrasting warm spots of light from the windows and their reflections in the water. Whistler's career spanning America, France and England, and his preoccupation with how he painted rather than what he painted, are both prophetic of the development of modern art.

James Abbot McNeill Whistler,
Nocturne in Blue-Green 1871

Albert Moore transformed the classicism of ancient Greece and Rome into something very new and individual through his interest in Japanese art. 'Blossoms' is characteristic of his work, and one of his most accomplished paintings. His primary inspiration was the sculpture of the Parthenon frieze but in the 1860s, together with his friend Whistler, he discovered Japanese prints. The two artists thereafter signed their paintings with symbols in the Japanese manner rather than with their names: Whistler with the famous butterfly, and Moore, significantly, with a classical anthemion. But it was the subtle use of line and shape and, particularly, the light and refined colours of Japanese prints that redirected the work of both artists. While Whistler concentrated mostly on portraits and especially the famous river scenes, Moore painted almost exclusively compositions of female figures. They have no narrative nor any specific subject; they are intended primarily to please the eye. Their titles, like Whistler's, are evocative rather than descriptive. Many of his pictures are of groups of figures disposed across the canvas in the manner of a sculptured frieze – the seated goddesses in the east pediment of the Parthenon in particular, and these seem to have inspired Whistler to paint works such as 'Three Figures: Pink and Grey' in the Tate collection, although Whistler's work is always less classical and more Japanese in spirit. Moore always retained his interest in antique sculpture, and aimed to fuse classical drapery, architectural details and sculptural monumentality with Japanese decorative patterns, ceramics and soft colouring. 'Blossoms' confines Moore to a single standing figure in the tradition of a classical Venus. She is fully draped, not in a toga, but in a loose-fitting robe, and she lifts her arms so her hands reach over her right shoulder to clasp the nape of her neck. This pose allows Moore to study fully the ripple of the folds of fabric. He diligently studied the drapery folds, making not only a full-scale cartoon for the whole composition but another for the drapery alone. The woman herself is designed in a gentle classical counterpoise, although her frankly direct gaze at the spectator is far from classical. The space behind her is hidden by a wall of the blossoms that give the picture its title, and there is a sprig of blossom at her feet. The most oriental aspect of the picture is the colouring. The soft pinks of the blossom pervade the delicate tonality of the whole painting, enhanced as so often in Moore's work by the use of pure white. It might well be called, in the manner of Whistler, 'Harmony in Pink and White'. Moore also exploits the creamy liquidity of oil paint, and the ease and grace of his brushwork conceal the study and effort behind his art.

Albert Moore
Blossoms 1881
Oil on canvas,
$58 \times 18\frac{1}{4}$ (147.3 × 46.3)

Impressionism and Post-Impressionism

In the National Gallery the Impressionist and Post-Impressionist pictures are exhibited as the most recent of the series of masterpieces of painting from the thirteenth to the nineteenth century; the Courtauld Gallery, Woburn Square, WC1, illustrates the taste of a great collector and his advisers in part of the same field. Many of the most important Impressionist and Post-Impressionist paintings formerly at the Tate were transferred to the National Gallery some years ago, and those few remaining form the essential background and the decisive starting point for twentieth-century art, which is now the main area covered by the Tate's modern collection.

The vast majority of the paintings and sculptures exhibited in the official salons of the time were illustrations of sentimental or erotic anecdotes in period or exotic settings, landscapes, portraits and still lifes, executed in a debased traditional style. The painters now called Impressionists and Post-Impressionists who attempted to find a new truth were derided, hated or ignored by all but a minority. They became, whether deliberately or incidentally, revolutionaries and most of the painters of the twentieth century have seen themselves, however different their styles and intentions, as the heirs to this continuous revolution. It has become, much more consciously than before, essential to a painter's achievement to be seen to have evolved a personal and original style, and the rate of specialisation, diversification and innovation has accelerated in the arts in a way that is comparable with the rate in the fields of science and technology. It is this which sets twentieth-century art apart from that of any previous period.

In the case of Impressionism the decision to try and achieve in paint the closest possible equivalent to what was actually seen led paradoxically to a first step towards abstraction, for the artists came to concentrate not so much on the objects themselves as on their sensations of light and colour, or, in terms of painting, on the separate brushstrokes of bright paint with which they tried to match them.

A comparison of Pissarro's 'The Pork Butcher', Sisley's 'The Path to the Old Ferry at By' and Monet's 'The Seine at Port-Villez' illustrates three degrees in this abstraction of light. Pissarro is clearly interested in the human and social implications of his subject. Sisley, if

Claude Monet, **Poplars on the Epte** 1891

only by his choice of subject, evokes the traditional townsman's sentiment towards the countryside, but Monet is concerned almost entirely with atmosphere and light. From about 1890 Monet even began to paint series of pictures of the same motif in different conditions of light and atmosphere, working on a number of canvases at the same time and switching from one to another as the conditions of light changed. 'Poplars on the Epte', though incorrectly dated 1890, is from a series of no less than twenty-three pictures of this particular belt of trees painted in 1891.

Among the Impressionist pictures still at the Tate is a group of works by Camille Pissarro, including his last self-portrait painted in 1903. The Gallery's only remaining painting by Renoir is a small portrait study of a girl, but there are also three of the sculptures which he modelled at the end of his life with the help of an assistant. Crippled by arthritis and unable to work the clay himself, he directed his assistant with the aid of a pointer. Nevertheless these works have rounded forms and a glowing, sensual vitality.

Degas, though he painted and modelled subjects like ballet dancers and circus performers, executed them with an almost complete emotional objectivity, studying the characteristic movements made by the models unselfconsciously in the course of their habitual or professional activities. In painting he often adopted arabesque-like compositions, cut off at the edges, so unusual as to draw attention to the fact that the viewpoint and consequently the appearance of the object in a picture is an entirely arbitrary choice on the part of the artist ('Woman at her Toilet'). This was perhaps a lesson learnt from Japanese prints and photography. He also extended his work into making sculptures of women and horses, though only one 'The Little Dancer aged Fourteen', wearing a real muslin tutu, was exhibited during his lifetime.

Degas' pastels of women bathing and drying themselves had some impact on Forain as in 'The Tub' *c.* 1886–7. Many of his later paintings were dark-toned courtroom scenes, a theme much used by Daumier.

The term Post-Impressionist is imprecise in meaning; invented by Roger Fry when organising the exhibition 'Manet and the Post-Impressionists' in London in 1910, it is often used to describe the work of Cézanne, Gauguin, van Gogh and Seurat.

Cézanne's early works were melodramatic and dark in tone, often painted with great violence with a palette knife, then in the early 1870s he began with the encouragement of Pissarro to brighten his colours and observe nature more closely. However, he later declared

that he wanted 'to do Poussin again, from nature' and that his aim was 'to make of Impressionism something solid and durable, like the art of museums'. His painting of 'The Avenue at the Jas de Bouffan', probably executed about 1874–5, already anticipates his later development as it is constructed in a series of zones parallel to the picture surface, with a compressed space, heavy forms and diagonal planes of foliage. Cézanne spent many years working in isolation trying to reconcile his perceptions with the relationships of touches of colour on the flat

Paul Cézanne, **The Gardener** 1906

picture surface. He found that every brushstroke affected all the others and, being unwilling to compromise his vision by adopting a ready-made style into which each detail could be inserted, he could never paint a complete picture on his own terms. He was forced therefore to select certain relationships of colour and form only. The unfinished 'Still Life with Water Jug' and the radically simplified 'The Gardener', painted shortly before his death bear witness to this. Cézanne understood that the appearance of the object changes as the eye moves over or around it. But it was as much his demonstration of the consequent impossibility of an optically objective painting as the techniques he devised to integrate the picture-surface, so that all the shapes on it were made to relate to one another and to the background, which led to Cubism and so to the abstract art of this century.

Edgar Degas, **The Little Dancer aged Fourteen** 1880–1

Paul Gauguin, **Faa Iheihe** 1898

Seurat tried to convert Impressionism into a scientific method. He systematically divided colours into their components: the colour of the object, the colour of the light which falls on it, reflections and the effects of placing one colour next to another, and he painted them all separately in small dots or streaks. He believed also that colours and lines produced a fixed emotional effect and that a picture could be constructed out of these in a planned way. 'Le Bec du Hoc, Grandcamp', 1885, which was one of his earliest coastal scenes, has a stylised linear outline akin to Art Nouveau; it includes a painted border in the complementary colours. 'Clothes on the Grass' is one of a series of *croquetons* (oil sketches on panel) done as studies for his large figure composition 'Bathing at Asnières' formerly at the Tate but now at the National Gallery.

Van Gogh and Gauguin, too, used colours to affect the emotions. Van Gogh's early works were dark coloured scenes of Dutch peasants and their life. After moving to Paris in 1886 he adopted the bright palette and techniques of Impressionism, then in 1888 set out for Arles in Provence, where he attained his characteristic mature style, with its blazing colours, rhythmical distortions and expressive brushwork. Subject to spells of intense elation and despair, he sought to convey his reactions to the world around him with as much urgency and directness as possible. 'Farms near Auvers' was painted in 1890 only a few weeks before his suicide.

Gauguin turned against the rationalism and materialism of his period and went to live in Brittany, Martinique and Tahiti, where he was moved by the simplicity and mystery of the way of life of the peasants and natives. He tried to find an equivalent for this in painting, using broad flat areas of sometimes arbitrary colour, simplified and evocative curving shapes and stylised gestures which he found in works of art that do not belong to the Western tradition. 'Harvest: Le Pouldu', 1890, was painted in Brittany the year before his first visit to the Pacific. 'Faa Iheihe', 1898, reflects his interest in oriental

art, in this instance Javanese sculptured friezes.

The Irish painter Roderic O'Conor lived at Pont-Aven in Brittany for most of the 1890s, and became a friend of Gauguin's. However 'Yellow Landscape, Pont-Aven', 1892, was probably painted before he met Gauguin himself and seems to show the influence of van Gogh, who had died only two years before.

The sombre-toned portrait of Emile Bernard painted in 1885 is one of Toulouse-Lautrec's finest early works. He later developed a rapid graphic style and a degree of caricature in his portraits and pictures of prostitutes, music-hall dancers and singers. Both the techniques and the subject-matter of these three, Lautrec, Gauguin and, above all, van Gogh, became the principal source of Expressionism in the next generation and since.

Working in isolation, the self-taught artist Henri Rousseau (often known as 'Le Douanier') painted pictures which despite an uncertain grasp of perspective, anatomy and so on, had a poetic character and a clarity of colour and form that recalls the Italian primitives. The full merits of his work only began to be appreciated

Roderic O'Conor, **Yellow Landscape, Pont-Aven** 1892

Henri Rousseau, **Flowers** *c.*1909–10

Auguste Rodin, **The Kiss** 1901–4

in the last years of his life, from 1906 onwards, and his first admirers and collectors included Picasso, Robert Delaunay and Apollinaire.

Auguste Rodin was the dominant force in sculpture at the end of the nineteenth century and the beginning of the twentieth, and most of the other leading sculptors either worked under his influence or reacted strongly against it. His very life-like figures, often depicted in movement, expressed a wide range of human emotions, including despair and erotic love. Most of his sculptures were modelled for bronze casting, and the bronzes tend to have an uneven, light-catching surface that relates them to Impressionism. He seldom carved marble himself and the marble versions of his sculptures, such as 'The Kiss', were usually carved by assistants working under his direction. Like many of his works, 'The Kiss' was an enlargement of a group originally intended for 'The Gates of Hell', a monumental sculptural portal commissioned for the Musée des Arts Décoratifs but never completed. The Tate's marble is a replica of the one now in the Musée Rodin in Paris and was executed in 1901–4 for the Anglo-American antiquarian Edward Perry Warren.

Intimists, Matisse and the Fauves

Aristide Maillol, **The Three Nymphs** 1930–8

The work of Bonnard and Vuillard was in a sense transitional between the nineteenth and twentieth centuries. Both began in the 1890s as members of the Nabi group, making flat, highly patterned pictures and prints, then in the early 1900s started to introduce more space and come closer to Impressionism. Vuillard's 'The Laden Table' painted about 1908 is a transitional work inasmuch as it already has considerable depth (one is very conscious of looking into the receding corner of a room), but retains a strong sense of pattern, with forms cut off abruptly by the edges of the composition. By about 1920 the treatment is much more conventional, as

in 'Sunlit Interior', in which the room is filled with sunlight streaming in through the open window.

Both Bonnard and Vuillard tended to concentrate on intimate subject-matter, middle-class interiors, informal nudes and portraits. Vuillard spent most of his life with his widowed mother, who appears in many of his pictures; Bonnard was also of a retiring disposition and liked to paint his immediate surroundings, with affection and tenderness, and sometimes not without a touch of humour. Most of Bonnard's early works depict Parisian scenes, as in 'Pont de la Concorde', 1913/15, but he later spent much of his time in the South at St Tropez, Le Cannet and elsewhere and was influenced by the intense Mediterranean light. His later paintings of nudes, interiors, landscapes and still life became increasingly rich in colour, with a luxuriant saturation of soft glowing colours.

The sculptures by Bonnard's friend Maillol, with their heavy forms and static poses, have a Mediterranean grace. His 'Three Nymphs' are grouped like the classical 'Three Graces', but have a warm and sensuous quality derived from life.

Whereas Bonnard stood for most of his life somewhat apart from the most avant-garde movements (though his late and most daring works had considerable influence in the 1940s and 1950s on School of Paris abstract painting), the work of the Fauves was regarded from the first as revolutionary and is usually considered to be the first important new movement in this century, and a vital link in the development of modern art.

The founders of Fauvism were Matisse, Derain, Vlaminck and Marquet, who came to know one another about 1898–1901, and they were joined about 1905–6 by Friesz and Dufy, among others.

'Nude Study in Blue' by Matisse, painted in 1899 or 1900 at the Académie Carrière (one can glimpse another painter at his easel in the background) is strongly influenced by Cézanne but is executed in a range of sombre, weighty blues, reds, greens and browns. In 'Notre Dame' of about 1900 the tonality is heightened and there is a wider range of pure colours. The movement at its peak is illustrated by three pictures: the portraits Matisse and Derain painted of each other at Collioure in the summer of 1905, and Derain's 'Pool of London'. They are all painted in broad brushstrokes and in brilliant colours which are sometimes arbitrary but more often a simplification and intensification of what is seen. Indeed, Derain hardly goes farther than this. Matisse's portrait of him is more radical; it employs sequences of similar and contrasting colours in the greens and reds which, because of the expressiveness and harmony of their relationship, seem to correspond more closely to something in the artist than in what he sees. Colour therefore becomes the subject of the painting as well as its expression.

Pierre Bonnard
The Bowl of Milk *c.*1919
Oil on canvas,
$45\frac{3}{4} \times 47\frac{5}{8}$ (116.2 × 121.6)

This picture was first exhibited at the Salon des Indépendants in 1920 as 'Interior', then at the Galerie Druet, Paris, in 1924 as 'Interior at Antibes' and at Rosenberg and Helft, London, in 1937 as 'The Bowl of Milk'. The setting is a room at Antibes and through the window can be seen the blue of the Mediterranean. A young woman in a pink dress standing on the right is holding a small bowl in her hand and is apparently preparing to feed the cat whose silhouette appears in the foreground. Sunlight streams through the window; light

falls across the table and laps around the figure of the girl. The rest of the room is filled with a muted glow of reflected light and shadow.

The girl's head is seen from its own level but one looks down on to the table and down still further on to the floor, so that the table top even seems to curl downwards towards one (a use of a shifting viewpoint probably derived from Degas), while the eye explores the space of the room, the spaces between objects and the distance back to the far corner. There are no hard outlines, but everything is softened by the light and the palpitating colour. A limited range of succulent colours is used all over the picture surface, soft touches of the complementary

colours introducing a suggestion of the shimmering vibration of the light.

This transformation of an everyday domestic scene, of something quiet and unspectacular but deeply felt – whether it be a figure in a room or people at table or a woman having a bath – is characteristic of Bonnard's work of this period. An apparent casualness conceals a masterly sense of pictorial construction, while the sensuous colour and all-pervading light give the pictures a strongly lyrical quality.

The Tate is fortunate to possess an extremely fine group of Bonnards of the period 1913–25, though as yet there is no example of his later work in which the colours attain a still greater luxuriance and saturation.

Fauvism owed much to van Gogh and Gauguin, and was partly based on the theory that colour and form can have a direct effect upon the feelings of the viewer almost without regard to what is represented. However, the Fauves were without the Messianic personalities of the two earlier painters and did not go to the same emotional extremes as the Expressionists.

Henri Matisse, **Standing Nude** 1907

Although Matisse's style evolved in later years, once in response to the rise of Cubism ('Standing Nude', 1907), and again to participate in the common return to a classicising naturalism in the twenties ('Reading Woman with Parasol', 1921), his method of painting remained fundamentally the same. Paradoxically, for a painter so deeply concerned with colour and light, it is best illustrated in the Tate by the series of bronze reliefs 'The Back' executed at intervals over a period of twenty years. He began with something seen and, step by step, working over the same motif again and again, each time using what he had done before as the starting point for the new relief, he simplified the image, making the formal relationships at once richer, more concise and more harmonious, until he reached the final statement which is never geometric but remains human, true both to his own feelings and to the model.

'The Inattentive Reader' of 1919, with its patterning, its clear luminous colour and its free yet precise drawing, is a characteristic work of his middle period. In his last years, when he was largely bedridden, he gave up easel painting and devoted most of his time to making cut-out gouaches in brilliant colours with the help of assistants. 'The Snail', 1953, which is discussed separately, is one of the finest and at the same time most abstract of these.

André Derain
The Pool of London 1906
Oil on canvas, $25\frac{7}{8} \times 39$ (65.7×99)

This picture, a fine example of Derain's Fauve period, depicts the Pool of London with Tower Bridge in the background, and was apparently painted from London Bridge.

According to a letter from the artist: 'This picture is of 1906. It was one of a group of pictures which I made for M. Vollard who had sent me to London at that time so that I could make some paintings for him. After a stay in London he was very enthusiastic and wanted paintings inspired by the London atmosphere. He sent me in the hope of renewing completely at that date the expression which Claude Monet had so strikingly achieved which had made a very strong impression in Paris in the preceding years.

'The majority of these pictures were among the canvases which he kept by him. He sold a few but many remained and were dispersed in the sales made by his heirs.'

The paintings by Monet to which Derain referred were the views of the Thames executed during various visits to London from 1899 to 1904 and exhibited in Paris in May–June 1904. But whereas Monet painted series of canvases of the same three motifs – Waterloo Bridge, Charing Cross Bridge and the Houses of Parliament – studying different effects of light and atmosphere, Derain moved his pitch almost every time, working at a number of points along the Thames from the Houses of Parliament to as far east as Greenwich (though he also executed several pictures in Regent Street and Hyde Park). This particular site, with its coming and going of shipping, evidently had special attraction for him, as at least four other oils are known of the view across the Pool of London to Tower Bridge.

The composition is obviously closely based on the actual scene, though with a certain degree of simplification, but the rather drab colours of the original are transposed into an exuberant range of glowing reds, blues and purples.

Expressionism

This is a term which is applied specifically to the styles of certain German groups of painters in the early part of the century, and more generally to describe tendencies that have always been present in art, namely the use of distortion and violent execution or colour to.express deep or violent emotions which cannot be communicated simply by painting what the eye sees.

One of the principal pioneers of twentieth-century Expressionism was the Norwegian painter Edvard Munch, who wrote in his notebook: 'No longer should you paint interiors with men reading and women knitting. There must be living beings who breathe and feel and love and suffer.' The Tate's 'Sick Child' is the fourth of six painted versions of this composition, the earliest of

Edvard Munch, **The Sick Child** 1907

which was made in 1885–6. The theme is said to have been inspired by the illness of his elder sister Sofie, who died from tuberculosis in 1877 at the age of fifteen. The emotionally highly charged atmosphere, the woman doubled up with grief, the child's pale face framed with red hair, is heightened by the strong, rather sour colour and the fretted brushstrokes which introduce a quivering vibration.

Something of the same rather frenzied atmosphere can be seen in the big picture by Lovis Corinth 'The Temptation of St Anthony' which was based on an episode in Flaubert's *La Tentation de St Antoine* in which St Anthony was tempted by the Queen of Sheba, who appeared before him with a train of exotic attendants, including an elephant and women astride piebald horses. The composition has a strong Old Masterly character, though the handling is in places quite similar to that of Manet.

Munch spent much of his time in Germany from 1892 to 1908 and had considerable influence on various German painters, including the artists of the Brücke group, Kirchner, Schmidt-Rottluff, Heckel, Pechstein, Otto Müller and Nolde. The group, which was founded in Dresden in 1906, was given the name Die Brücke (The Bridge) to signify that it was intended to serve as a bridge between the old art and the new. It was to some extent the German equivalent of the Fauve movement in that the artists tended to use strong colours and to be greatly attracted by African and other primitive art, but their work usually has a more neurotic character and is rougher in form, with a preference for broken colours rather than clear pure primary colours. Schmidt-Rottluff's 'Two Women' of 1912 shows some influence of Gauguin's paintings of Tahitian women but is considerably more distorted, while his 'Woman with a Bag' painted three years later has a heavily stylised head related to negro wood sculpture. Kirchner's 'Bathing at Moritzburg', begun about 1910 and largely repainted in the early 1920s, depicts the artist and his friends nude bathing in the open air, and is executed in a range of blues, greens and greenish orange which evoke the warm sunlight. Nolde, who only belonged to the group for a short time, is represented by the seascape discussed separately.

Michel Larionov, **Soldier on a Horse** *c.*1911

Emil Nolde
The Sea B 1930
Oil on canvas, 29 × 39¾ (73.7 × 101)

This picture has been exhibited
since 1956 with the dates 1915–17 or
1915–20, but it is in fact one of six
seascapes entitled 'Sea A–F' which
were painted in 1930 on the island of
Sylt. Nolde went to stay there in the
summer of 1930 while his new house
at Seebüll was being repaired and
found accommodation at Kampen
with a window overlooking the
North Sea.

As he recorded in his memoirs
Reisen – Ächtung – Befreiung 1919–
1946 (Cologne 1967): 'I had a wish

to live and paint as alone as possible,
only observing, and in particular I
wanted to see the sea once again, in
all its wild greatness . . .

'Months went by, that would have
tried many men. Time passed quite
quickly. I had remained almost completely alone. Autumn had arrived,
the days grew shorter. Thunder-
clouds came, driven by hail-storms –
lightening flashed into the sea . . .

'I had finished or almost finished
six seascapes, whose paint was still
wet, working on them in a state close
to ecstasy and contemplating and
assessing them over and over again.'

Much of Nolde's work is concerned with imaginative or religious
subjects, and there is often a strong
influence of the stylisation and

dramatically barbaric character of
African or Oceanic art. Though
there is a kind of savage wildness in
this picture also, this is combined
with very close observation of the sea
under storm conditions – the surge
and fall of the sea, the foaming white
crests of the waves, the turbulent
storm clouds borne along by the
wind and the strange yellowish light
breaking through from behind the
clouds. Though Nolde joined the
Brücke group briefly from 1906 to
1907 he was essentially a visionary
who chose to spend the greater part
of his life working in isolation, from
1927 until his death in 1953 mainly
at Seebüll, in a remote part of
Schleswig-Holstein close to the
Danish border.

George Grosz, **Suicide** 1916

Oskar Kokoschka, **View of the Thames** 1959

Other examples of German Expressionism are the Gallery's works by Grosz, Beckmann, Barlach and Lehmbruck. The painting 'Suicide' by Grosz was executed in Berlin in 1916. Bitterly opposed to the war, which filled him with disgust and aversion for mankind, he drew and painted drunkards, sadistic murderers, prostitutes, war cripples and suicides. The sprawling body of the dead man with a revolver beside him is contrasted with the half-naked prostitute and her drunken client at a nearby window, while a further corpse hangs from a lamp-post; pedestrians and dogs scurry past in a furtive manner. Beckmann's 'Prunier' was painted in 1944, during the Second World War while the artist was living in Amsterdam trying to keep out of the way of the Nazis, and conveys a strong sense of unease. The heavy black outlines, the mysterious figures guzzling seafood and the ambiguous adjuncts such as the lampshade and the arrow carry overtones of drama and menace. The sculpture by Barlach, swathed in loose drapery reminiscent of early Gothic art, is compact and intensely dramatic, while the head by Lehmbruck has an air of gentle melancholy. On the other hand the Belgian, Constant Permeke, who was the leading figure in the Flemish Expressionist movement, used painting conventions somewhat similar to those of the Brücke artists to depict the life of peasants and fisherfolk: simple robust

people living close to nature. The rich earthy colours and monumental simplifications raise his pictures to the level of heroic grandeur.

Oskar Kokoschka, the greatest painter of Central European Expressionism, is represented by three relatively late pictures, all executed after 1938 when he arrived in this country as a refugee. Two of them – the landscape of Polperro in Cornwall and the portrait of the Soviet Ambassador Ivan Maisky – were painted during the Second World War, while the panoramic view of the Thames was done in 1959 in the course of one of his return visits to London, after he had gone to live in Switzerland. Executed from the roof of the Shell-Mex building next to the Savoy, and looking down the river towards St Paul's, this landscape is one of a series of more than a dozen views of London which he painted at intervals over the years.

Maurice Utrillo, **La Porte Saint Martin** *c.*1910

Rouault and Soutine were Expressionists in the general sense of the term. Though Rouault exhibited briefly with the Fauve painters (several of whom had been fellow pupils of his at the Atelier Gustave Moreau), he never really belonged to the group but was essentially a religious artist with a tragic vision. His early painting 'The Bride (Aunt Sallys)', which depicts a wedding group with the bride between her parents, was based on the life-size aunt sallys which one finds in fairs and is obviously a savage comment on bourgeois standards, while in his own words 'The Three Judges' embodies the anguish which he felt 'at the sight of a human being who has to pass judgement on other men'. 'The Three Judges' is painted in a style influenced by his own early experiences as assistant to a restorer of medieval stained glass, with heavy black lines and rich, glowing areas of

The paintings by Utrillo – usually either views of Paris or of provincial churches – are quieter and more elegiac and were mostly executed from picture postcards. Comparison with the actual cards used shows that Utrillo kept closely to the main lines of the original, but simplified and purified the forms. A busy, crowded street scene would become almost deserted; buildings would appear to be empty; tonal contrasts would be heightened. In this way they were transposed into a poignant expression of his own loneliness and melancholy, and a kind of yearning for a state of ideal purity.

Soutine, Utrillo and Modigliani all belonged to the circle of bohemian artists in Montmartre whose lives were plagued with poverty and alcoholism. Modigliani, who was an Italian Jew by origin, concentrated mainly on sculpture in 1910–14 before developing his characteristic painting style. He had begum to make sculpture under the influence of Brancusi and his elongated head is one of a series of very stylised carvings on this theme. His later paintings, which are almost all either portraits or nudes, tend to have a rhythmical linear stylisation. 'The Little Peasant' was probably executed in the South of France, at Cagnes or Nice, and is one of the most Cézanne-like of all his works.

Georges Rouault, **The Three Judges** c.1936

colour. The faces are akin to caricature but of a most powerfully expressive kind. The Tate's three pictures by Soutine are all landscapes, in which the scenes are convulsively twisted and distorted by the violence of his own emotions. Although the Céret landscape, which is the earliest and most extreme, has sometimes been known as 'Storm at Céret', the stormy effect is to be seen rather as a projection of his own anguish than as a rendering of the weather; the hillside appears to be caught up in a violent earthquake or a whirlwind.

Amedeo Modigliani, **The Little Peasant** 1919

British Art 1880–1920

Stanhope A. Forbes, **The Health of the Bride** 1889

From about the time of the Pre-Raphaelites many young British artists were dissatisfied with the Royal Academy and thought much of the art exhibited there to be dull and lifeless. From the 1860s more and more artists looked to France for a lead but, apart from isolated exceptions such as the Irishman Roderic O'Conor, they tended to know surprisingly little about the most advanced art being produced there. Nevertheless they often developed qualities of intensity, freshness or eccentricity which were very much their own. Ideas originating in Paris were to dominate innovations in British art until the middle of the twentieth century.

Impressionist paintings were exhibited in London in the 1880s with little success, though a few artists responded warmly to their light and colour. A more typical reaction was that of the painter of 'Derby Day', W.P. Frith: 'A new style of art has arisen, which seems to gratify a public ever craving for novelty . . . the *bizarre* French "impressionist" style of painting recently imported into this country will do incalculable damage to the modern school of English art.' Such hostile receptions were to characterise exhibitions in Britain of art in new idioms time and time again, from Post-Impressionism to Abstract Expressionism, Minimalism and beyond.

Painting out-of-doors as practised in France by Bastien-Lepage at least gained supporters in the 1880s, such as George Clausen, as well as leading to the formation of the 'Glasgow School' and the 'Newlyn School'. Stanhope Forbes, one of the principal artists of the latter, was delighted by Cornwall because there 'the figures did not clash with the sentiment of the place' and he could paint both together. 'The Health of the Bride' was executed using the artist's friends as models and the setting was a local inn. Forbes was mainly interested in genre subjects, but 'A Hopeless Dawn' by another Newlyn painter, Bramley, shows the persistence in the group of more dramatic ideas. In some respects these pictures are still the 'quiet scenes of humour or pathos' noted by Thackeray earlier in the century. The idea of art for its own sake which Whistler publicised did not become current until the next century.

John Singer Sargent, an American trained in Paris and a friend of Monet from the early 1880s, developed a bravura portrait style owing much to his admiration for Hals and Velazquez. 'Carnation, Lily, Lily, Rose' combines a Pre-Raphaelite subject with loose, Impressionist handling of paint.

The one painter working in England who shared the initial French impetus towards Impressionism was the cosmopolitan James McNeill Whistler. Whistler's influence was widespread, greatest perhaps on interior decoration, and many cleared their living rooms of Victorian bric-à-brac and replaced closely patterned with simpler, lighter wallpaper. It also created the climate of taste in which Aubrey Beardsley could make his intensely individual contributions to Art Nouveau in black and white.

John Singer Sargent, **Carnation, Lily, Lily, Rose** 1885–6

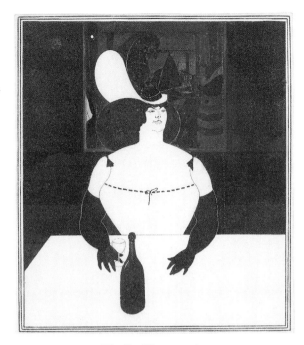

Aubrey Beardsley, **The Fat Woman** 1894

Among painters Walter Greaves, who started as an untaught 'primitive' artist, and Paul Maitland were perhaps Whistler's closest disciples with their pictures of the Thames and nearby streets. The rococo arcadian fantasies, often painted on fans, and views of the seaside of Charles Conder owe something to Whistler's delicacy in handling paint, though are lighter in tone. They also reflect Conder's admiration for the work of Puvis de Chavannes.

The paintings of James Pryde and William Nicholson, who as young men collaborated in producing graphic work under the name of the Beggarstaff Brothers, echoed Whistler's subtlety. Pryde's sombre dramatic style was at root romantic and traditional; Nicholson's work was by contrast naturalistic, but it possessed a delicate and lovely precision that reappeared in the work of his son Ben.

The Impressionist preoccupation with light emerged fully into English art in the work of Wilson Steer and Walter Sickert. The delicate boldness of Steer's early seaside canvases actually anticipated the trend of painting in France, but closer knowledge of Impressionist methods and admiration for the great pre-Impressionists, Turner and Constable, led to a progressive weakening. Sickert began as a pupil of Whistler and in France he was in touch with Degas, but the personal quality of his work never wavered in his career of sixty years. He looked at the charms of common life and the tinselled lustre of things with an affection that was mixed with ironic detachment, as if to nourish a suspicion that the aim was really his delight in painterly deftness for its own sake and the pristine glitter of pigment.

Philip Wilson Steer, **Boulogne Sands** 1888–91

Augustus John, early renowned as a fluent draughtsman and for whom facility was always a danger, was trained at the Slade School and never lost the dash and directness that it gave him. But the little pictures that he painted in the company of a fellow Welshman, J.D. Innes (until the latter's early death), reflected the positiveness of Post-Impressionism and a clear-eyed yet romantic feeling for a wild simplicity of life and landscape. Thereafter John, a prolific and often candid portraitist, was at his best when least calculating the bravura effects of paint. The art of his sister, Gwen John, was more secluded and private. Painting single figures of girls or women in circumscribed designs with a limited tonality, she represented human solitariness with a gravity and ultimately a piety not often within the reach of modern painting.

Sir William Nicholson, **Mushrooms** 1940

In 1910 and 1912 Roger Fry organised two exhibitions of Post-Impressionist art in London, the first mainly featuring Manet, Cézanne, van Gogh and Gauguin, and the second including major works by Matisse and the Cubists. Futurist paintings were also on view elsewhere in London in 1912, 1913 and 1914. These exhibitions appalled the public and presented younger artists with a mass of aesthetic ideas that could not be ignored. A feeling of a sudden exhilarating expansion of aesthetic possibilities can be detected in most British avant-garde painting for the rest of the decade; the variety of styles, sometimes even within the work of one artist over a short period, reflected the sudden concentrated and rapid exposure to so many developments.

The artists of the Camden Town Group, which began to form around Sickert after his return to England from abroad in 1905 and which also included Lucien Pissarro, the eldest son of Camille, tended to react to these exhibitions by heightening their colour and using broader paint areas without departing from their original subject matter based on a direct representation of the ordinary scene. One Camden Town painter, Robert Bevan, had met Gauguin while working at Pont-Aven in 1894. In his mature work this influence shows indirectly in the urge to simplification and in rhythms – albeit angular rather than curved – especially apt in his paintings of horses in

Harold Gilman, **Canal Bridge, Flekkefjord** c.1913

the town. A similar tendency towards broad handling of form appears in Spencer Gore's work, notably in 'The Cinder Path' depicting the outskirts of the then recently built garden city of Letchworth. In Gilman's later work, such as his portrait of Mrs Mounter or 'The Canal Bridge', detailed compositional discipline joins with heightened colour and tactile paint texture consciously derived from van Gogh. The same influence was adopted

Augustus John, **The Smiling Woman** c.1908

Gwen John, **Self Portrait** c.1899–1900

Walter Richard Sickert
Ennui *c.*1914
Oil on canvas,
60 × 44¼ (152.4 × 112.4)

Most of the paintings of Walter
Richard Sickert are concerned with
people and their urban environment.
A pupil of Whistler and a disciple of
Degas, Sickert was an actor before
studying briefly at the Slade. Many
of his early works are scenes of
London music halls and their audi-
ences and the theatre were to provide
him with subjects all his life. Above
all Sickert found a poetry in the
seedier parts of North London,
Dieppe and Venice and the life of
their inhabitants.

Up to the latter part of the first
decade of this century Sickert
painted with a dark, almost sombre
palette of browns, greys and blacks
relieved by a few highlights. Also,
unlike the French Impressionists,
he often painted from studies and
carefully squared-up drawings and
then applied pigment in a dense
impasto.

Various of his pictures are an
exploration of the relationship
between man and woman, both in
the bedroom and downstairs, but
the situations they depict tend to be
ambiguous and he would sometimes
give similar compositions
completely different names: for
instance, a nude woman lying on a
bed on which sits a clothed man
could be entitled 'What shall we do
for the rent', 'Summer Afternoon'
or even 'The Camden Town
Murder'. The title of this one,
'Ennui' (Boredom), is more explicit.

'Ennui' is Sickert's best known
work and exists in at least four other
versions, all considerably smaller
than the Tate's picture for which
two were painted as rehearsals. The
models were 'Hubby', a childhood
friend of the artist, who afterwards
ran away to sea, and Marie Hayes,
Sickert's maidservant.

The compositional tension of the
painting, with large areas of undecor-
ated wall and bare table, reflect and
enhance the mood of psychological
tension and boredom projected by
the two characters, who may or may
not be husband and wife or father
and daughter.

In an essay published in 1934
Virginia Woolf described Sickert as
being 'a novelist' in his paintings:
'The figures are motionless, of
course, but each has been seized in a
moment of crisis, it is difficult to look
at them and not to invent a plot, to
hear what they are saying. You
remember the picture of the old
publican, with his glass on the table
before him and a cigar gone cold at
his lips, looking out of his shrewd
little pig's eyes at the intolerable
wastes of desolation in front of him?
A fat woman lounges, her arm on a
cheap yellow chest of drawers, behind him. It is all over with them one
feels. The accumulated weariness of
innumerable days has discharged its
burden on them.'

Duncan Grant, **The Tub** 1912

Idiosyncratic interpretations of the human figure were developed by several artists who were students together at the Slade School, notably William Roberts, Mark Gertler and Stanley Spencer. Roberts was from the first preoccupied with the tense interaction of groups of figures. In his work from the 1920s onwards, figures engaged with a fierce concentration in some group activity are arranged in increasingly closely packed complexes, which reveal Roberts' intricate organisational gift. The figures grew rounder in the 1930s, but without losing a mannequin-like stiffness and stylisation. Roberts shared with Gertler and Spencer an intermittent tendency to tilt the ground plane steeply. For Gertler it was one of several means to his central aim of giving nature permanence and solidity on the canvas. His methods were successively, precise realism, doll-like simplication, adaptations of Cézanne, and – his principal style of the 1920s and early 1930s – a predilection for heavy, dense forms with a hot, almost over-mellow colour range.

Stanley Spencer minutely observed the matter of a strange but simple daily existence, and reordered it in imaginative episodic paintings which express the mystical experience real life embodied for him. A powerful intuitive dramatic sense gives a disconcerting quality to the events he painted with great directness. In the 1910s especially, these have in their simplicity almost the feeling of visions: he was then already representing biblical episodes taking place in his own time in the landscape of his Berkshire village of Cookham, which had for him a special concentrated intensity analogous to that of the Shoreham Valley for Palmer (with whose early self-portrait Spencer's in the Tate may be compared).

by Charles Ginner in a personal style even more precise and condensed which he maintained over forty years.

Though the most radical and sustained innovations were those made by the Vorticists and their associates (whose work is discussed separately under the heading 'Vorticism'), the variety of possibilities which were opening to British painting before the First World War are exemplified by the versatility of Duncan Grant. Whatever the form, he preserved the sensitive richness of colour that was natural to him. Like Vanessa Bell he responded most to the work of Matisse, but 'The Tub' reflects something of the impact of Picasso and African sculpture.

The Fauvist example of the freedom of colour was strongly followed by Matthew Smith who had studied briefly under Matisse: the emphatic and surprising structure of his early landscapes and nudes indicates the connection, as does his predilection for maximising the area of each block of colour. Thereafter his paint became increasingly succulent and freely worked, the brilliant and vigorous colours saturating the canvas area to create an emotional and plastic intensity close to continental Expressionism. Smith's controlled extravagance continued for fifty years to give to traditional subjects a force that made Francis Bacon one of his admirers.

Sir Matthew Smith, **Cornish Church** 1920

Sir Stanley Spencer
Swan Upping 1914–19
Oil on canvas,
$58\frac{1}{4} \times 45\frac{3}{4}$ (148 × 116.2)

The son of a builder and church organist, Stanley Spencer was born in Cookham-on-Thames, Berkshire, where he spent most of his life. Because he travelled to London each day while studying at the Slade from 1908–12 he was nicknamed 'Cookham' by his fellow students. Much of Spencer's painting relates to Cookham and Biblical subjects. The

large 'Resurrection' 1923–7, for example, is depicted occurring in Cookham churchyard.

'Swan Upping' is an annual event each August when officials of the companies of Vintners and Dyers, who by Royal Licence own the swans on the River Thames, take up the young birds for marking. The picture shows the swans being brought ashore in carpenters' bags outside Turk's Boat House near the Ferry Hotel, Cookham. Spencer thought out the composition partly in Cookham Church, where he could hear boats being hauled in and out of the river, and the sound of oars. In this way he imagined the scene as very wonderful and linked to a religious background. He did not wish to be dominated by outside influences so he made no studies by the river, but painted a small study from imagination. The picture was started in 1914–15, when about the top two thirds was done, and then finished in 1919 after he was demobilised from the army.

The painting has an air of heightened reality, and the light reflected from the water suggests moonlight yet events take place in the foreground in daylight. The mood of anxiety seen in the immobilised swans and the face of the woman on the bridge is enhanced by the serrated edges of the clouds and the flame-like branches of the tree on the right. An ordinary scene is made to appear extraordinary.

The pattern of the sides of the cast iron bridge is echoed in the covers of the cushions carried by the woman on the right. In later years Spencer was to exploit more and more the pictorial possibilities of the patterning of clothes and other textiles.

Cubism

The pictures of Picasso's first personal and original phases, the Blue and Pink periods, with their mood-creating colours and emotive distortions ('Girl in a Chemise', c.1905, 'Boy with a Horse', 1905–6) are akin in method to the earlier phases of Expressionism. It was probably, therefore, his search for force of expression which led him to take an interest in primitive sculptures, first those of the Iberian peninsula and then of Africa, but their formal freedom and concision became one of the main sources of his Cubism.

In spite of its short duration Cubism has remained the most important and influential movement of the twentieth century. This is true both because the artists associated with it took some of the most decisive steps towards abstraction and because it appeared so extreme that it has become the archetype of all later revolutionary movements.

Pablo Picasso, **Girl in a Chemise** c.1905

Following up hints which they had discovered in the work of Cézanne, the creators of Cubism, Picasso and Braque, attempted to replace single viewpoint perspective, which had been normal in Western art since the Renaissance, with a procedure which involved an attempt to combine many aspects of an object into a single image and thus to give a more complete representation of it. The problem which faced them was how to put all these features on to a flat canvas and the emphasis was therefore removed from the object itself and placed on the technique and on the organisation of the picture surface. Colours were temporarily abandoned, shapes were simplified and flattened and space was rendered by means of oblique lines and overlapping forms. Subjects had to be simple and familiar so that it would be possible to read them through the complexities of the style.

In 1909 Picasso and Braque each painted a few Cubist landscapes, but for several years thereafter they restricted their subject matter to single figures, including in Picasso's case a few portraits, and above all still lifes of bottles, glasses, sheet music, musical instruments and a few other objects normally found in their studios or the cafés they visited.

This crucial phase, from about 1908 until early 1912, usually known as analytical Cubism, is illustrated by two Picassos, three Braques and a Gleizes. The Picassos, painted in the period 1909–10, are both of the seated figure. 'Bust of a Woman' shows block-like forms with clearly defined facets and is influenced by African wood sculpture. In 'Seated Nude' the facets have become slightly disengaged from each other and there are several instances of a changing viewpoint, particularly the downward view on the model's right shoulder and breast and the upward view of her left; at the same time the figure is still more or less detached from the background. The three pictures by Braque are still lifes and are close in style to Picasso's work of the same period but, as always, more sensuous and less deliberately shocking. They show slightly later stages in the development of analytical Cubism: there is a much shallower picture space and an interlocking of objects and background, so that the facets flow into one another. 'The Guitar' is not attacked and dismembered like Picasso's subjects, but delicately evoked in terms of a system of zig-zagging planes displaced from the motif.

Albert Gleizes, who was one of those who joined the Cubist movement in 1909–10, painted his monumental 'Portrait of Jacques Nayral' early in 1911. He belonged to a different group of Cubist artists centred round Passy, on the outskirts of Paris, which also included Marcel Duchamp, Jacques Villon and the sculptor Duchamp-Villon. Instead of having all the forms fragmented and integrated with the background plane, as in Picasso and Braque's works of the same date, it depicts a nearly life-size figure rendered with sculptural solidity

Georges Braque
**Clarinet and Bottle of Rum on a
Mantelpiece** 1911
Oil on canvas,
$34\frac{1}{2} \times 23\frac{3}{4}$ (87.6 × 60.3)

The close collaboration between
Braque and Picasso in the development of Cubism reached its peak
when they spent the summer of 1911
together at Céret in the French
Pyrenees. There they painted some
of their most important and
magisterial analytical Cubist
pictures, some nearing total
abstraction. The works which they
painted at this time are often difficult
to tell apart, though Braque's
handling of paint has a more
sensuous painterly character.

'Clarinet and Bottle of Rum on a
Mantelpiece', which was painted at
Céret, has a linear framework of
verticals, horizontals and inter-
secting diagonals, combined with
stippled areas of paint applied in
short stabbing strokes. References to
the visible world are few: there is a
bottle at the top with a clarinet
behind it and towards the bottom
two scroll-like corbels, left and right,
which apparently serve to support
the mantel. At the extreme bottom,
towards the left, is a scallop shape
which is probably either the handle
of a firescreen or part of a canopy at
the top of the fireplace to prevent
smoke escaping. Objects are broken
down into geometrical shapes and
several different characteristic
aspects of the same object are
sometimes combined together. For
instance the main part of the clarinet
is seen from the side but the bell is
painted as if viewed from the back,
so that it is almost circular; the
right-hand corbel is viewed first
from one side and then from the
other so that it has the appearance of
twisting. Forms overlap and merge
into one another; planes, sometimes

partly transparent, are flattened and
superimposed. The picture space is
very shallow like a low relief, and the
colours are almost monochromatic,
restricted to a narrow range of ochres
and greys. Braque has brought in
further references to the 'real' world
by the use of stencil-like letters,
without which the composition
would be much more difficult to
read; they help to identify the bottle
and the piece of sheet music. There
is also an illusionistically painted pin
whose shadow shows it to be illuminated from the left, whereas the rest

of the imagery is predominantly lit
from the right.

This picture, which belonged for
many years to Le Corbusier, illustrates a crucial moment in the
development of Cubism, when the
breaking down of objects had been
carried to a point very close to
complete abstraction. Soon afterwards Braque and Picasso began to
introduce areas of wood-graining
and then to work with collage, so as
to bring back colour into painting
and to represent objects in a more
recognisable but symbolic way.

Juan Gris, **The Sunblind** 1914

crucial historical importance for they are the origin of all contemporary sculpture which is built rather than modelled, and that relies on the enclosure of a void. They had great influence on the Constructivist movement in particular. Pure colours first began to make their re-appearance in Cubism in the series of paintings by Robert Delaunay, 'Windows open simultaneously', painted in 1912. Later phases of Cubism are often rich in colour contrasts and strongly patterned.

Ozenfant, Le Corbusier and particularly Léger show a reaction away from traditional art subjects and pre-occupations, and an interest in machines and machine-made objects. Léger aimed to produce a style clear, direct, objective and as representative of the machine age as the product of a lathe. His images are as simple and clear-cut as if they had been produced by a stencil. Four paintings illustrate his mature style in the twenties, while the 'Two Women holding Flowers' of 1954 shows the device of separating colour from form and also the change of orientation in his last period from inanimate objects to people.

Cubist works were exhibited in several major European cities, as well as New York in the years between 1910 and 1913, and artists in a number of countries including Germany, Holland, Hungary and Czechoslovakia were influenced by Cubism. In Russia among others Malevich, Larionov, and Nathalie Gontcharova ('Linen', 1913) painted works in a Cubist idiom.

The influence of Cubism in sculpture can be seen in the relief 'The Lovers', 1913, by Raymond Duchamp-Villon, and the 'Cubist Bust' by the Czech sculptor Oto Gutfreund; in 'Woman combing her Hair' by Archipenko, and in the early sculptures by Jacques Lipchitz, particu-larly his semi-abstract 'Head' of 1915. In making 'The Horse' in 1914, Duchamp-Villon began with the theme of a horse and rider poised at the moment of preparing to leap, and gradually transformed this image through a

and seated in the open air surrounded by trees, plants and houses. Though there is a good deal of depth in places, the background is densely packed with forms which seem to be caught up in a restless, flickering movement.

By the summer of 1911 and early 1912 Braque and Picasso had carried Cubism almost to the point of complete abstraction; 'Clarinet and Bottle of Rum on a Mantelpiece', 1911, by Braque has a few clues, the bottle and clarinet, the scroll-like corbels supporting the mantelpiece, though it would be more difficult to 'read' without the commercial lettering. The introduction of lettering and imitation wood graining, together with the much greater flatness of the compositions, led to the flat planes being replaced by cut-out paper and the re-introduction of colour. Objects such as pieces of wall-paper or newspaper could be physically incorporated into the picture. This technique, known as collage, calls into question the relationship of image to objects and, differently used, became one of the key procedures of Dada and Surrealism. Picasso's 'Bottle of Vieux Marc, Glass, Guitar and Newspaper', 1913, and Gris's 'The Sunblind', 1914, are good examples. 'Still Life', 1914, by Picasso is one of the rare and important reliefs which he made in 1912–14 as an extension of his synthetic Cubist paintings and collages. These sculptures are of

Pablo Picasso, **Still Life** 1914

Fernand Léger
Still Life with a Beer Mug 1921–2
Oil on canvas,
$36\frac{1}{4} \times 23\frac{5}{8}$ (92.1 × 60)

Among the great twentieth-century masters, Léger stands out for his peculiarly modern dynamism. In many ways his pictures anticipate the preoccupations of all contemporary artists who set out, through the use of strong colour and clear-cut shapes, to make a powerful visual impact on the spectator. This is not surprising, since Léger's art was addressed to the widest possible audience and both in subject matter and technique sought to reflect the vitality and energy of our modern industrialised world. His images have the precision of machine forms.

In this picture the everyday ingredients of a workman's lunch, a beer mug, plates and fruit, are grouped together on a table top, which is tilted towards us. A blue curtain frames the composition on the right-hand side. There are indications of a window at the top right, while the floor appears to be tipped vertically downwards, parallel to the picture plane, so that the diamond floor-covering forms a black and white repeat pattern. The rest of the background is crowded with an extraordinary variety of patterned areas of an apparently arbitrary kind, a black disc inside a white square, a small criss-crossed rectangle like a flag, and so on. The red, white and blue beer mug with its large handle occupies the centre, the focal point of the composition and appears to be floating in front of the other forms instead of standing firmly on the table. The composition is built up in a series of layers, one behind another.

The inscription 'Etat définitif' on the back of the canvas indicates that this was the final version of this composition and a pencil drawing and a smaller, sketchier oil painting apparently represent preliminary stages. They show that Léger began with a somewhat more realistic treatment (for instance with the diamond floor pattern set at an angle to suggest recession) and step by step made a number of adjustments to the distribution and balance of the contrasting patterns, so that the composition became progressively more and more precise and vibrant. This enhanced those features which appear to anticipate, to a degree exceptional in his work, both the Op Art of Vasarely and the Pop Art of Roy Lichtenstein.

Robert Delaunay, **Windows open simultaneously (first part, third motif)** 1912

Raymond Duchamp-Villon, **Large Horse** 1914

series of studies into a dynamic fusion of the horse and machine forms.

The lesser Cubist painters and sculptors continued the style after it had been largely abandoned by Picasso and Braque, about 1924, though the collection also contains three pictures painted by Braque in 1925–7 in which some of the ideas of Cubism are still found. But they are mainly concerned with the exploitation of colour and texture in paint.

After the 1914–18 war Picasso, in common with a number of other artists, turned partly to a kind of neo-classicism which combined to some extent the formal interests of the previous decade with those of a representational idiom based on Ingres, Poussin and Greek sculpture. It is represented here by 'Seated Woman', 1923. However, his period of neo-classical calm soon gave place to the frightening series of pictures with which he reacted to crises in his personal life and to the political events of the inter-war years.

The Tate is fortunate to have from this period one of those major works which Picasso painted every few years and which seem to inaugurate or sum up a new development. This is 'The Three Dancers' of 1925. The tortured style, with its violent distortions, marked the beginning of Picasso's Surrealist period.

Among the pictures of the following decades are series of works which are comparable in intensity but which are lyrical and erotic almost without any quality of anxiety and hysteria. These celebrate his relations with women and are remarkable for the way in which he evolved a new style to treat each person. One of these is 'Nude Woman in a Red Armchair', 1932, with its looping voluptuous curves. Like almost all his later pictures it contains Cubist idioms, in this case his frequent combination of full-face and profile in the head.

The act of choosing an expressive style is an essential part of Picasso's art and he continued to invent styles and explore new media until the end of his life. The Gallery's only postwar painting is a still life, 'Goat's Skull, Bottle and Candle' painted in 1952, in which black and white and a convolution of curved and angular lines give the motif a quality of obsession and anxiety.

Pablo Picasso
The Three Dancers 1925
Oil on canvas,
84¾ × 56 (215.3 × 142.2)

'The Three Dancers', one of Picasso's key works, was painted in 1925 at a crucial moment in his development, and marks the beginning of a new period of emotional violence and Expressionist distortion.

The starting point for this picture seems to have been three dancers rehearsing in a room in front of a pair of french windows. The central figure is much the least distorted, but even so her body is very thin and elongated and has an almost ghostly, insubstantial quality. The right-hand figure, on the other hand, is divided into clear-cut, contrasting areas. A strange feature is that the brown section surmounted by a tiny, helmet-like head is entirely surrounded and engulfed by another, much larger black head of a completely different character. Much the most extraordinary dancer, however, is the one on the left, who dances with a much more frenzied action than either of the others and seems to flaunt her sexuality. Particularly remarkable is the rendering of the head which combines a frontal view that is savage and mask-like with a further image of a profile like a crescent moon that is gentle and dreamy in expression.

A clue to this strange picture is provided by a remark of Picasso's in 1965: 'While I was painting this picture an old friend of mine, Ramon Pichot, died and I have always felt that it should be called "The Death of Pichot" rather than "The Three Dancers". The tall black figure behind the dancer on the right is the presence of Pichot.' The Spanish painter Ramon Pichot died in Paris on 1 March 1925. His death seems to have reminded Picasso of an incident which took place as long before as 1901 and which inspired several paintings by him at the time, namely the tragic suicide of the young Catalan painter Carlos Casagemas. Casagemas accompanied Picasso on his first visit to Paris in 1900, where he became obsessed with a girl named Germaine. Overcome by depression, thinking only of suicide, he first fired a revolver at Germaine but missed, then shot himself in the head. Germaine married Ramon Pichot shortly afterwards.

It would appear that after Pichot's death, the picture took on various deeper meanings – a sort of Dance of Death, with Pichot on the right, Germaine on the left, and Casagemas like a crucified figure between them.

Futurism

Giacomo Balla,
Abstract Speed – The Car has passed 1913

Among the movements which developed out of Cubism, Futurism was founded in Italy by the poet Marinetti. Unlike the previous movements it was propagandised in words, as well as paintings and sculpture, by the artists themselves who were deliberately and aggressively revolutionary. The aim of the Futurists, as expounded in their founding manifesto of 1909, was to destroy the art of the past, which was particularly oppressive to young painters in Italy, and to substitute for it a new art based on speed, violence and machines. 'We declare that the world's splendour has been enriched by a new beauty: the beauty of speed . . . a roaring automobile, which seems to run like a machine-gun, is more beautiful than the *Victory of Samothrace*.'

In the technical manifesto of the following year the painters claimed that 'movement and light destroy the materiality of bodies'.

The Futurists took over certain techniques from Pointillism and later from Cubism, but instead of using a shifting viewpoint which moved around the object like the Cubists, they depicted objects which were themselves in movement. This was usually conveyed by successive multiple images (probably derived from photography). In his late Futurist painting 'Suburban Train arriving in Paris', 1915, Severini suggests movement by a series of parallel bands of smoke and fragmented, thrusting planes. Movement could also be depicted in a more abstract way as in Balla's 'Abstract Speed – The Car has passed'. The work of Umberto Boccioni, the leading painter and sculptor of the group, illustrates the other principal aim of the movement which was to project feelings, or as he called them, 'states of mind', by colour and the rhythm of lines and brushstrokes. But in his sculpture 'Unique Forms of Continuity of Space' he celebrated the powerful muscular dynamism of the striding human figure in a way which combines traditional sculpture with the spatial discoveries of Cubism.

Umberto Boccioni,
Unique Forms of Continuity in Space 1913

Vorticism

Vorticism, which aimed at a synthesis of Cubism and Futurism, originated about 1912 but was not established as a clearly defined movement until 1914 when the American poet Ezra Pound invented the term 'Vorticism', Wyndham Lewis founded the Rebel Art Centre as a rival to Roger Fry's Omega Workshops, and the Vorticist manifesto was published in the first of two numbers of the magazine *Blast*. Members of the group included Wadsworth, Roberts, Gaudier-Brzeska, Atkinson, Hamilton, Jessica Dismorr and Helen Saunders. Lewis was the leading spirit and polemicist of Vorticism; the style of his manifestos and his writings in *Blast*, no less than the paintings and drawings, expressed the critical spirit of aggression inseparable from the movement as a whole.

Emphasising the anti-realistic character of their art

Wyndham Lewis, **Workshop** *c.*1914–15

the Vorticists represented the human figure and its surroundings in a jagged, rhythmical and linear style, which also included many works of near or total abstraction. Formally the angular predominated over the curved, the hard over the soft, the precise over the undefined; colour was used with more concern for pictorial than representational necessities. The work of the Vorticists was aroused by and hoped to propagate taut, powerful mechanistic forms and a pervading vitality in modern society; a dynamic principle was, they felt, common to both. Man-made forms, products of human intelligence, must discipline nature, which they would exclude. The Vorticists' concern with vigour and energy in life and their belligerent tone of voice was close to that of the Futurists, from whom they derived much. (Marinetti

William Roberts, **The Cinema** 1920

visited England several times in 1910–14; Nevinson, who was associated with the Vorticists, called himself a Futurist and published the manifesto 'Vital English Art' jointly with Marinetti in 1914; Nevinson's painting 'The Arrival' *c.*1914, is close in style to Severini). They rejected however the Futurist's means of representing movement as too Impressionistic, as inimical to hard clarity of form, and the contents as too descriptive.

Vorticist imagery is above all crisp, and in its short unified period it shows frequent analogies with architectural form, especially in the works by Lewis and Wadsworth. Some of the most ambitious oil paintings produced by the Vorticists have disappeared, and their work is known mainly from drawings and watercolours. The Tate's representation of the movement, which is unique in its comprehensiveness, includes Lewis's only two known surviving Vorticist oils: 'The Crowd', *c.* 1915 and 'Workshop', the latter suggesting architecture of the modern city.

The one sculptor member of the Vorticist group was the mercurial Henri Gaudier-Brzeska, born in France, who spent almost all his life as an artist in England. In four years he produced forceful work in a great variety of styles, from the lyrical naturalism of the 'Dancer', the African Primitivism of 'The Imp', the facetted 'Cubic' (Gaudier's own description) bust of Horace Brodzky, to the humorous semi-abstraction of 'Bird swallowing Fish'. Gaudier's work has a controlled energy which emerges in his pastels where the colours are hot and non-naturalistic, and in the nervous vital lines of his drawings of animals and people.

The impetus of Vorticism as a coherent development was dissipated, somewhat ironically, by the First World War. Gaudier-Brzeska was killed on the Western Front at the age of twenty-three; the other Vorticists and their associates developed in different directions. Wadsworth was to reappear as an abstract painter and as a Surrealist. Etchells translated Le Corbusier's *Towards a New Architecture* and became an architect. Epstein turned increasingly to modelling and portrait sculpture. Bomberg, like Epstein, developed an Expressionist idiom which he applied in an increasingly forceful and gestural way to paintings of landscape, flowerpieces and portraits.

The most direct continuation of Vorticism was in the work of Wyndham Lewis. Although after the war he repudiated the abstract tendencies of the 1910s, he achieved in both portraits and paintings of figures in settings a distinct, concentrated tightly sprung quality. This derived partly from his strange adaptation of Cubist and Futurist idioms, with a cursive touch and curling lines giving to solid form an undulating character playing against static mass. Lewis also conjured up fantastic and alien environments peopled by mutations of men, animals and machines.

Sir Jacob Epstein, **Doves** *c.*1913

The American-born sculptor Jacob Epstein was associated with the Vorticists but was never actually a member of the group. Many of his early works were concerned with procreation and fecundity like 'Female Figure in Flenite', 1913; the 'Doves', *c.*1913, perhaps the most abstract of all his carvings, suggests the copulatory motions of a pair of mechanical birds. His one important work close in spirit to Vorticist ideals was 'Rock Drill', 1913–15, a ferocious, visored machine-like image which when originally shown stood ten feet high when mounted on an actual pneumatic rock drill. David Bomberg, like Epstein, was not a member of the Vorticist group but his two major pictures of 1913–14, 'In the Hold' and 'The Mud Bath', suggest agitated human movement by means of a fragmented patterning of great vitality.

David Bomberg
The Mud Bath 1914
Oil on canvas,
66 × 88¼ (167.6 × 224.2)

David Bomberg painted 'The Mud Bath' when aged twenty-three, a year after leaving the Slade School of Art. The subject was inspired in part by the sight of bathers in a small pool at a steam (not mud) baths in White-chapel near Bomberg's home in the East End of London.

The picture projects above all an image of violent movement, with figures apparently running, diving or falling into, or standing in a pool. The vertical column gives stability to the composition which consists almost entirely of straight lines in jagged, staccato rhythms, with very few curves. Colours are restricted to the red pool surrounded by the yellow floor, contrasted with the white highlights and blue shadows of the figures, and the maroon column with its black shadow. The figures are reduced to geometrical shapes which are just sufficient to suggest human beings.

The abstract shapes between the figures are almost as important as the figures themselves. The eye is pulled backwards and forwards between seeing the painting as one of figures in violent motion and as abstract shapes remorselessly fighting one another for supremacy.

From the examples of Cubism, Futurism and the works of some of those artists who were to call them-selves Vorticists, Bomberg created in this painting something uniquely his own.

When 'The Mud Bath' was shown in Bomberg's first one-man exhibi-tion in July 1914 it was hung on the outside wall of the gallery. In the catalogue the artist wrote 'I appeal to a *sense of form* . . . I look upon *nature* while I live in a *steel city*. Where decoration happens, it is accidental. My object is the *construction of pure form*'.

Despite praise from a few critics the exhibition was a failure. 'The Mud Bath' was stored in a garage for several decades and almost for-gotten, and was not exhibited again until after the artist's death when it and Bomberg's 'In the Hold' were recognised as being perhaps the most important English paintings of their time.

Abstract Art up to the Second World War

Wassily Kandinsky, **Cossacks** 1910–11

As early as the 1850s Delacroix wrote that, if the colour in a painting has been used successfully, when one stands at a distance too great to identify the subject, one should get the feeling of the painting, whether gay, melancholy or violent, from the colour alone. Clearly by then it was inevitable that one day artists would ask whether it was necessary to have a subject at all. A growing emphasis in the late nineteenth and early twentieth centuries on the expressive qualities of colours and shapes, combined with a tendency on the part of many artists to attach less and less importance to subject-matter, culminated in a widespread development of abstract art about 1910–15.

Wassily Kandinsky, who was born in Russia but was then working in Munich, is usually said to have made his first abstract work – a watercolour – as early as 1910. However most of his paintings for several years afterwards still contained residual subject-matter evocative of Russian fairy tales and folk lore. For example the Tate's early picture 'Cossacks' of 1910–11 (sometimes known as 'Battle' or as 'Fragment of "Composition IV"') includes two cossacks on horseback duelling with sabres, a castle on a hill, a party of birds in flight and three more cossacks on the right, two of whom hold lances. Nevertheless the main emphasis is on the dynamic and expressive arrangement of colours and lines, which he used in a manner analogous to music. Heavy black lines surge to left

and right, there are clashes of movement, and a rainbow-cum-bridge brings together all the colours in the painting.

Whereas Kandinsky approached abstract art by way of Fauve colour and Expressionism, other artists took as their starting point Cubism which had been carried by Picasso and Braque in 1911 to a point very close to complete abstraction (though traces of objects were always deliberately retained). The Dutchman Piet Mondrian felt that the logical culmination of this tendency was complete abstraction and in 'Tree' of c.1912–13, which was probably the last but one of his series of paintings of trees, almost all traces of the original image have been eliminated. Painted in a delicate range of soft greys and ochres, and in a style still clearly indebted to analytical Cubism, it becomes an image for contemplation of an almost mystical kind, related to his own interest in Theosophy. In the top

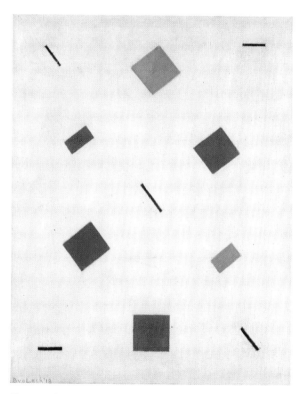

Bart van der Leck, **Abstract Composition** 1918

section of the painting one can already see signs of a preoccupation with a more rectilinear structure which was to become characteristic of his next phase. In 1916 he met Bart van der Leck who had begun to paint very simplified figure compositions with flat planes of the three primary colours; and in 1917–18 van der Leck himself painted a few completely non-figurative works under the title 'Mathematical Image'. The Tate's picture of 1918 is probably one of these and is based on a

Piet Mondrian
**Composition in Grey, Red,
Yellow and Blue** 1920–c.1926
Oil on canvas,
39¼ × 39½ (99.7 × 100.3)

There is still no work in the Tate's collection to show how Mondrian began as an orthodox landscape painter in the Hague School tradition, and then came under the successive influences of Fauvism, Symbolism and Cubism, but the Gallery's three pictures by him are representative of particularly crucial stages in his development from 1912 onwards. The earliest is 'Tree' of 1912–13 which comes at the moment – a turning-point in his art – when he was carrying Cubism over into complete abstraction.

The picture reproduced here is signed and dated 1920 but was probably not completed until several years later, as it appears in two photographs of Mondrian's Paris studio taken about 1925 in an apparently unfinished state. It is one of the largest of a related group of seven canvases dated from 1919 to early 1921 in which he used larger

rectangles than before and with black, several different shades of grey, and the three primary colours mixed with grey. The square canvas is divided up into rectangles, some aligned vertically and some horizontally. The colour blocks are distributed asymmetrically, sometimes in groups of twos or threes, but nevertheless the picture is brought into a state of perfect balance and harmony. Thin black lines mark out the divisions of the picture surface but only play a minor part in the effect.

These particular pictures formed an important stage in the transition to Mondrian's later, most characteristic abstract work because of their complete flatness, the division of the picture surface into a number of relatively large rectangles, the vertical-horizontal structure, the emphasis on primary colours and the use of a linear grid. However, Mondrian then went on to eliminate

grey and to work with a white ground divided up by a rectilinear grid of heavy black lines and with one or more rectangles of pure, saturated red, yellow or blue – that is to say, using elements of maximum contrast.

The latest of the Tate's pictures, 'Composition with Red, Yellow and Blue', is dated 1939–42 but is now known to have been begun slightly earlier, about 1937. It was therefore worked on over a long period and was begun in Paris, probably continued while he was living in London from 1938 to 1940, and finished after his move to New York. The grid of black lines is the dominant element (the points where the lines intersect taking on an almost Op Art dazzle), while the blue and red stripes towards the bottom relate to his very last pictures, in which he began to work with coloured stripes instead of black ones.

Kasimir Malevich, **Dynamic Suprematism** 1915–16

carefully balanced composition of rectangles or bars of red, yellow, blue and black widely distributed along vertical, horizontal and diagonal axes on a white ground; all suggestion of depth is avoided so as to emphasise the flatness of the picture plane. A similar tendency is apparent in Mondrian's 'Composition in Grey, Red, Yellow and Blue', 1920–c.1926 in which the picture surface is entirely divided up horizontally and vertically into rectangles of various sizes. Mondrian, van Doesburg, van der Leck and a few others founded in 1917 the abstract movement known as De Stijl and published a periodical of the same name. Though the artists involved were mostly Dutch, they were joined by among others the Belgian painter and sculptor Georges Vantongerloo, whose 'Interrelation of Volumes' of 1919 was one of the first attempts to carry the principles of De Stijl into three dimensions. Carved in sandstone, it is rectilinear and block-like in structure without any reference to natural forms, closer to architecture than to any previous sculptures. In fact the group included not only painters and sculptors but architects such as Oud and designers such as Rietveld, who were concerned with giving the principles of De Stijl a practical application.

The earliest abstract movement in Russia itself was Rayonism, which was founded by Larionov in 1912. It was indebted both to Cubism and Futurism and was based on the interaction of the rays of light emanating from objects. For example his painting 'Nocturne' (which is signed and dated 1910 but was almost certainly made several years later, about 1914) was inspired by a twilight scene at Odessa, with the interiors and exteriors of houses and the interaction of the semi-light rays and the dark rays. However Larionov and his common-law

wife Gontcharova left Russia in 1915 and turned their attention thenceforth mainly to the ballet.

Altogether more radical than Rayonism, and of far wider significance outside Russia, was the movement known as Suprematism which was founded by Malevich in 1915 as an assertion of the absolute autonomy of the work of art, its complete independence from any form of representation of nature. It was based entirely on the use of flat geometric forms of contrasting colours on a white ground. 'Dynamic Suprematism', which dates from 1915–16, is typical in that the rectangular, triangular or circular elements appear to be floating at different intervals in depth and to be clustering together or drifting apart. It differs from De Stijl pictures both in its dynamic character and in that it is constructed in a series of layers instead of being completely flat.

Knowledge of the work of Malevich and of the principles of Suprematism was first carried to the West several years after the Revolution by Lissitzky, who lived in Germany and Switzerland from 1921–5. Some influences of both De Stijl and Suprematism can be seen in the work of the Hungarian Moholy-Nagy and the German Vordemberge-Gildewart at about this period.

Laszlo Moholy-Nagy, **K VII** 1922

Another abstract movement which originated in Russia at this time (for the years immediately before and after the Revolution were a period of extraordinary intellectual ferment in Russia) was Constructivism, which was based on the use of abstract forms and an enthusiastic acceptance of new materials and new methods of construction made available by modern technology. Naum Gabo, one of the founders, who published his Realistic Manifesto in Moscow in 1920, had begun in 1915 to make sculptures using a stereometric method of construction. His first pieces such as 'Head No. 2', 1916 (of which the Tate possesses a monumental enlargement made in 1964)

Naum Gabo
Head No. 2 1916
(enlarged version 1966)
Cor-ten steel,
$69 \times 52\frac{3}{4} \times 48\frac{1}{4}$ ($175.3 \times 134 \times 122.7$)

Gabo made the original Heads Nos.
1 and 2 to prove to himself and his
friends in Norway, where he was
then living, that the system of open
construction which he had derived
from the three-dimensional models
made by physicists and mathema-
ticians could be applied to any image
and in particular to a traditional
subject such as the human figure.
'Constructed Head No. 1' was made
in 1915 first in cardboard and then in
plywood. He considered that it was
only a partial success as it was in-
sufficiently concave, especially in the
lower section, so he went on to make
'Constructed Head No. 2' which he
felt embodied his ideas completely.
The starting-point for it was a char-
coal drawing of 1916 which depicted
a woman in a hat with a veil, though
the hat and veil are omitted from the
sculpture itself.

The sculpture is built out of
pockets of space, with the metal ribs
springing from a central axis. There
is only a single convex element – a
curved plane forming the figure's
right shoulder – and even this is not
closed. He set out to combine several
different aspects of the same image
so that, if one moves around the
sculpture to the left (that is to say, to
the figure's right), the head seems to
turn also, until seen from the side
there is another complete face looking towards one. This effect is not
repeated however on the other side,
which only has a profile view.
Although there are certain simi-
larities to analytical Cubism, Gabo
said that he regarded his aims, to
create in terms of space, as completely different.

'Constructed Head No. 2' was made
first in cardboard and then $17\frac{3}{4}$ inches
high in galvanised iron, which he
later covered with yellow Ripolin as
a protection against rust. It was
included in a major exhibition of
recent Russian art shown in Berlin in
1922, but was sent back to Russia
after the exhibition closed instead of
being returned direct to the artist,
who had decided to settle in Berlin.
He then completely lost trace of it
for over thirty-five years until it was
brought out of Russia about 1964.

As the yellow paint had begun to
come off, creating a very ugly
surface, he thought it best to remove
it. This enlargement was made in
1966 in Cor-ten steel (a steel widely
used for building purposes which
rusts but is self-sealing) and he later
made two further versions the same
size: one in Cor-ten steel of a slightly
different thickness and one in
stainless steel. He told the Tate it
was his intention from the beginning
to carry out this sculpture on at least
this scale.

were still based on the human figure but from 1917 onwards his work was completely abstract. He became greatly interested in the use of different kinds of plastics, sometimes strung with nylon threads, to create transparent sculptures of an extraordinary ethereal delicacy. Shortly before he died he presented to the Tate almost all the surviving maquettes for his most important sculptures, constituting a veritable anthology of his work, as well as several finished pieces to add to the works already in the collection, so that the Tate now possesses the most comprehensive representation of his work in any museum.

Vanessa Bell, **Abstract Painting** *c.*1914

Many of the pieces have a rhythmical configuration related to geometrical forms, such as his series of works on the 'Spheric Theme'. His brother Antoine Pevsner, who had begun as a painter and was co-signatory of the Realistic Manifesto, also turned to sculpture with great success but showed a preference for welded metal sculpture. Both artists left Russia in the years 1922–3 and moved first to Berlin, then to Paris. However Gabo subsequently lived from 1935–46 in England and finally settled in the United States.

In Britain also there were a few artists who made abstract works in the period 1913–15, notably certain painters of the Vorticist group such as Wyndham Lewis and Edward Wadsworth. Even Vanessa Bell, Roger Fry and Duncan Grant of the rival Bloomsbury circle made isolated experiments with abstract art at this time, though in a style closer to synthetic Cubism. Vanessa Bell's abstract painting of about 1914 reproduced here

has flat rectangular planes of rich, glowing colour, while Duncan Grant made a long scroll-like abstract collage of block-like forms rhythmically arranged which was intended to be mounted on rollers and to move past the viewer to the accompaniment of music (which, if it had been carried out, would have made it perhaps the very first kinetic work). However all these artists soon returned to figurative painting and very little further abstract work was produced in this country until the early 1930s when Ben Nicholson, Barbara Hepworth, Henry Moore and John Piper attempted to bring British art into the mainstream tradition of European abstraction. Mondrian, Gabo and Moholy-Nagy were among the major foreign artists who came to live here at this time for varying periods.

Whereas Vantongerloo, Gabo and Pevsner all made sculpture which was completely non-figurative, Brancusi usually took some simple theme such as a head, a bird or a fish as his starting point, and simplified and purified the forms more and more until he sometimes arrived at a point close to complete abstraction. The Tate's two bronzes 'Danaide' (which is one of the series of studies of Mademoiselle Pogany) and 'Maiastra' are still immediately recognisable as a head and a bird respectively, but most of the details have been eliminated and there is an

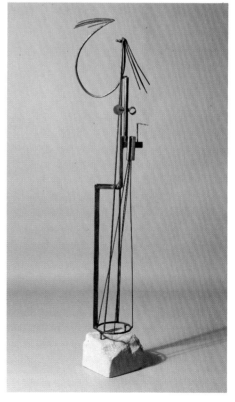

Julio Gonzalez, **Maternity** 1934

This bird is closely related to Brancusi's earliest sculpture of a bird, the white marble 'Pasarea Maiastra' in the Museum of Modern Art, New York (Pasarea = majestic, Maiastra = bird), and is believed to have been made from a plaster cast taken from the marble when it was still in an unfinished state. It belonged for many years to the famous American photographer Edward Steichen, who saw it for the first time at the Salon des Indépendants, probably in 1911. 'It appealed to me immediately', he wrote afterwards, 'as the most wonderful concept and execution I had seen by any sculptor with the exception of Rodin.' Brancusi helped to install it out of doors in the garden of his home in Voulangis, near Crécy-en-Brie, placing it on top of a square post of timber about ten feet high. It then had a much simpler double base consisting of a rectangular pillar of stone only slightly wider than the wooden post, surmounted by a small stone block of rectangular or possibly cylindrical form on which the bird gave the appearance of perching. The present base, shaped rather like a Romanesque capital and with two stylised profiles of birds carved on the front in low relief, was substituted later and is thought to have been carved, at least in part, by Brancusi himself.

The earliest Bird sculptures by Brancusi, including this one, were all inspired by the Maiastra or Pasarea Maiastra, a magic golden bird in Romanian folklore noted especially for its marvellous song, which had miraculous powers. (The Russian form of this same legend was the inspiration for Stravinsky's *Firebird*.) Here the bird's head is thrown back and its beak open as if it is in the act of singing. His later Birds became progressively more and more abstract and simplified until they turned into the theme of the 'Bird in Space', a slender, subtly curved shaft of marble or polished bronze. Altogether twenty-eight completed Birds are known, dating over a period of at least twenty-five years, and a twenty-ninth exists in the form of a shaft of marble on which the carving was only just begun. They are almost all slightly different, as the product of an endless process of simplification and refinement.

Constantin Brancusi
Maiastra 1911
Polished bronze, $21\frac{7}{8}$ (55.6) high on a stone base

emphasis in each case on the smooth rounded surfaces and on basic volumetric forms such as an ovoid. Some of his later bronzes and carvings are much more simplified, but it is only in his works of a more decorative or architectural character such as his 'Endless Column' that he broke with the representation of nature completely.

The sculpture of Julio Gonzalez is likewise difficult to classify, as it has links with abstract art, Cubism and Surrealism. Though he began his career as a metal-worker and as a painter and draughtsman (the Tate owns an extensive collection of his drawings of all periods), his most significant work was done after 1929 when he began to make welded iron sculpture under the influence of Picasso. 'Maternity' is a fine example of his open linear metal sculpture, like drawing in space, and is based on the theme of a mother and child treated in a highly abstracted way. As the main pioneer of welded iron sculpture, his work had great influence on David Smith and many other later sculptors.

Though some artists who had been pioneers of abstract painting turned to more figurative styles in the 1920s (Robert Delaunay and Malevich are examples), a number of other painters and sculptors joined the movement from 1930 onwards and close ties were formed between abstract artists working in different countries. The society 'Abstraction-Création' for instance, though founded in Paris in 1931, came to include abstract painters and sculptors working in Germany, Belgium, Italy, Poland, the USA and Great Britain. The painting 'Ile de France' by Hélion, executed in 1935, is typical of the pure clean-cut forms and clear colours favoured by most members of the movement. Robert Delaunay himself returned to complete abstraction in 1930 and painted a number of pictures, some very large, with abstract colour discs. In his 'Endless Rhythm' the coloured discs strung out diagonally across the picture are so arranged that each one leads on to the next and the movement is directed back again into the picture at the two ends. Kandinsky, Mondrian and Vantongerloo were among those who continued to develop their earlier styles with great authority.

Jean Hélion, **Ile de France** 1935

Dada, Surrealism and Fantastic Art

Marc Chagall, **The Poet Reclining** 1915

A tendency towards fantasy and the use of images derived from the unconscious is found in the art of many periods and the Surrealists themselves have claimed such artists as Bosch, Archimboldo and Goya among their forerunners. However the discoveries of psychoanalysis in this century, and particularly of Freud, have made modern man much more aware of the irrational impulses which influence our behaviour, and above all the power of the sex drive, the inventiveness of dreams and the loaded, ambiguous character of much imagery which is seemingly innocent. As soon as the Cubists and Expressionists had broken down the façade of visual appearances, the way was open to abstraction, but also to the inner world of association and dreams.

Chagall's mind was filled with memories of his childhood in the Jewish quarter of a provincial town in Russia. Gravity does not exist in his pictures, scale is free from the conventions of perspective and things appear by the magic of poetic association. 'The Poet Reclining' (Chagall himself) was painted in 1915 on the honeymoon

of his intensely happy marriage to Bella. A great many of his pictures were to celebrate their love, and after her death he finished 'Bouquet with Flying Lovers'. The association of white flowers, the little town of Vitebsk where they had met and lived, the crowing cock and the rich transparent blue are full of nostalgia and tenderness.

The most influential pioneer of both Dada and Surrealism was, however, the Italian artist Giorgio de Chirico, who began about 1912 in Paris to paint a series of dreamlike evocations of Italian piazzas, with colonnaded buildings, trains puffing smoke in the background and long cast shadows. The Tate's earliest example of his work is 'The Melancholy of Departure', which is one of his metaphysical pictures painted at Ferrara in 1916 when he was serving in the army but was able to continue painting in his spare time. It combines three quite different themes: a glimpse of an Italian piazza with a high building like a tower, an intricate 'scaffolding' made up partly of draughtsman's instruments such as a T-square and a triangle, and a map with a dotted line indicating a sea voyage. There is no rational explanation for this strange juxtaposition of images (or at least none is known), but they exert a mysterious, compelling fascination.

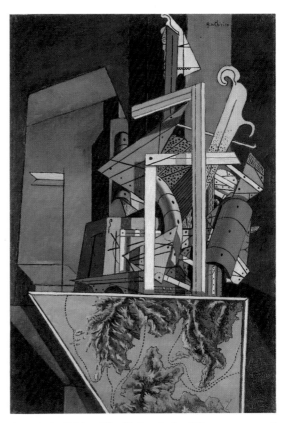

Giorgio de Chirico, **The Melancholy of Departure** 1916

Another very important pioneer of these tendencies was Marcel Duchamp, who is represented by a reconstruction of the large glass 'The Bride stripped bare by her Bachelors, even' which is his masterpiece. Duchamp made the original in New York in 1915–23, but it was accidentally smashed while being returned from an exhibition in 1926 and was not pieced together until ten years later; it is now in the Philadelphia Museum of Art. The reconstruction was made in 1965–6 by Richard Hamilton for inclusion in the exhibition he was organising of 'The Almost Complete Works of Marcel Duchamp' and took exactly a year to complete. The glass incorporates

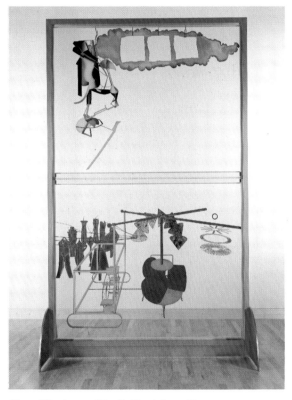

Marcel Duchamp, **The Bride stripped bare by her Bachelors, even** 1915–23, reconstructed by Richard Hamilton in 1965

various themes which had preoccupied Duchamp from 1912 onwards, with the bride in the upper section and in the lower part the nine malic moulds or bachelor machine, the slide, the water mill, the scissors, the sieves, the chocolate grinder and the oculist witnesses. Various notes made by the artist and collected together and published under the title *The Green Box* provide a key to this work which can be interpreted as a diagram of a love-making machine. Its ironic and erotic character is reinforced by the depiction of humans as fantastic machines.

During his stay in New York from 1915–18 Duchamp helped to launch a movement there akin to Dada which was joined by Picabia, Man Ray and Jean Crotti, among others, but the official Dada movement (Dada being the French word for hobby-horse, which was chosen at random from a dictionary) was founded in Zurich in 1916 by a group of artists and writers headed by the poet Tristan Tzara. Founded at the height of the First World War, it was both a gesture of utter rejection of accepted values which had brought the world to this state of catastrophe and an affirmation of new creative possibilities. The Dada movement quickly spread to other countries and in Berlin took on a left-wing revolutionary character in the savagely satirical work of George Grosz, John Heartfield and Raoul Hausmann (Hausmann's photomontage 'The Art Critic' is a violent attack on bourgeois prejudice and corruption), while in Cologne, Hanover and Paris the emphasis was more on the artistic side. Kurt Schwitters, for instance, founded in Hanover a personal variant of Dada known as Merz, based on the use of rubbish materials to create works of beauty by collage or assemblage.

Standing outside both Dada and Surrealism but greatly admired by the Surrealists was Paul Klee, a highly original artist of exceptional fantasy and wit. Even though his drawings may sometimes be based on those of

Paul Klee, **They're biting** 1920

Max Ernst
Celebes 1921
Oil on canvas,
$49\frac{3}{8} \times 42\frac{1}{2}$ (125.4 × 108)

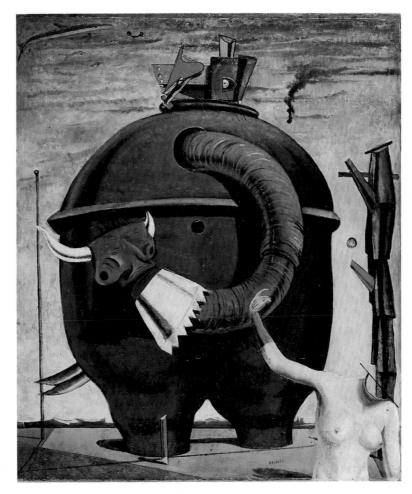

'Celebes', or 'The Elephant Celebes' as it is sometimes known, was painted in Cologne in 1921 and was Max Ernst's first large picture. It grew directly out of Ernst's use of collage from 1919 onwards to produce bizarre combinations of images, though no preliminary collages or sketches were made for it. The idea of the painting appeared spontaneously on the canvas with few alterations as it progressed. There are numerous light-hearted scribbles on the back, but none has any relation to the picture itself.

The boiler-like monster to which the title refers is, like the rest of the painting, highly ambiguous. It has a horned head with apparently sightless eyes, but a pair of tusks projecting on the left suggests the possible presence of a second head (or perhaps the real head?) on the other side. Its neck seems to consist of a long snake-like coil which emerges from a hole in its upper section; the top is surmounted by a brightly coloured construction containing a mysterious eye. It seems to be standing in a large open space, but there are also indications that it is embedded in a solid background, while two fishes swim in the sky above. Three upright objects stand around it, while in the bottom corner a headless mannequin figure with a raised arm appears to be beckoning the monster towards it.

Ernst confirmed that the image of the boiler-like form on its pair of 'legs' was originally inspired by an illustration in an English anthropological journal of a huge communal corn-bin peculiar to the Konkombwa tribe of the southern Sudan. The photograph is taken from the same angle and is basically very similar, but the artist has given the hollow clay container a metallic appearance and changed its character completely by adding the various appendages described above.

The title 'Celebes' was taken from some scurrilous couplets popular among German schoolboys, which begin:

The elephant from Celebes
has sticky, yellow bottom grease...
Usually regarded as the first major Surrealist painting (though it precedes by three years Breton's Surrealist manifesto of 1924) it is a haunting and disturbing image, which evokes among other things the nightmarish menace of the lumbering tanks and instruments of destruction of the First World War.

children and psychotics his wit is intensely sophisticated. For instance, 'A Young Lady's Adventure' depicts a fashionable lady nonplussed by the demonic spirits of nature, while 'They're biting', with its exclamation mark, is a humorous comment on his fishing expeditions with his young son. At the same time his work is formally extremely inventive in its line, colour and texture, and draws upon all the painterly idioms of the twentieth century. Usually small in scale and often in watercolour, his pictures are executed with extraordinary delicacy and subtlety.

Max Ernst, who founded with Arp the Cologne Dada group, became in turn one of the key members of the Surrealist movement. 'Men shall know Nothing of This' was painted in the year before the official founding of Surrealism in 1924 with a manifesto by the poet André Breton, but it already exemplifies many of the key ideas. It has been shown to be directly related to a specific psycho-analytical case-history which greatly interested Freud and which he discussed in papers of 1911 and 1923, the famous Schreber case upon which he based his theory of paranoia. The enigmatic combination of imagery, with its strongly erotic character, derives mainly from this source. The result is like a diagram of

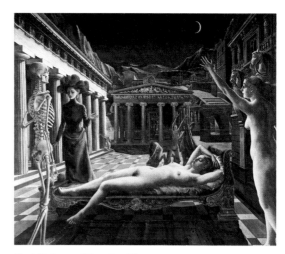

Paul Delvaux, **Sleeping Venus** 1944

the contents of the unconscious, the precision of the style reinforcing the strangeness of the imagery; but Ernst was to try to give complete freedom to the unconscious itself in his automatic paintings. Like the poets he found it impossible to put aside conscious control entirely, but 'The Forest' and 'The Entire City' show how the rubbing technique which he devised produced luxuriant and evocative forms that could be turned into a forest by the addition of a bird or into a fortified city by a ring which somehow represents the moon.

These two styles of Surrealism, the one in which a precise academic technique gives an air of verisimilitude to what is essentially subjective, and the other in which a degree of suspension of conscious control produces often abstract but still disturbing signs and images, remain constant in Surrealism. Magritte and Dali exemplify the former tendency. Most of Magritte's work is based on the depiction, in the most neutral manner possible, of some conventional bourgeois theme which is given a disturbing unreality and dead-pan humour by arbitrary changes of scale, by irrational juxtapositions of images and other such modifications. For instance, 'The Reckless Sleeper' at first glance consists of two unrelated parts: the enigmatic sleeping figure in his strange box and the group of familiar objects embedded in a slab of what appears to be lead, seen against a night sky. It seems likely, however, that the lower part represents the dream of the sleeper (and indeed some of the imagery, read in Freudian terms, is erotic).

Whereas Magritte took images from everyday life as his starting point, Dali's paintings are mostly of extravagantly fantastic scenes painted in a highly realistic, photographic-like technique. 'Autumnal Cannibalism', for instance, depicts two strange bulbous, viscous beings in the act of devouring one another with knives, forks and spoons. The action takes place on a chest-of-drawers

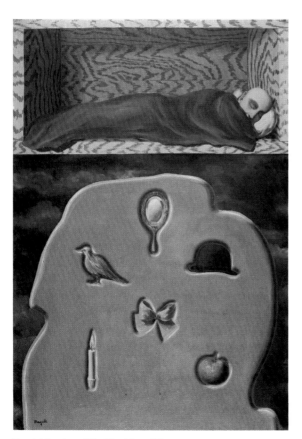

René Magritte, **The Reckless Sleeper** 1927

which turns into a beach, with a view of Dali's native region of Ampurdan in the background. Crawling ants, a crutch, a loaf of bread and an apple poised on the head like the one used by William Tell as a target are typical of the obsessional imagery which recurs in his work. The theme of two figures eating each other has an evident sexual connotation, but apparently also refers to the outbreak of the Spanish Civil War in July 1936, as Dali is reported to have said of this picture: 'These Iberian beings mutually devouring each other correspond to the

Salvador Dali, **Autumnal Cannibalism** 1936

pathos of civil war considered as a pure phenomenon of natural history.' Similarly 'Mountain Lake' is one of a small series of paintings with telephones inspired by Chamberlain's phone calls to Hitler, which culminated in the Munich Agreement of 30 September 1938. The pond is a double image, as it is also in the shape of a fish. 'The Invisibles' by Tanguy is painted in a technique similar to Dali's, but depicts a mysterious grouping of biomorphic or stony forms in a desert-like space.

Miró is the most distinguished of the more abstract Surrealist painters. The elements of his pictures are created sometimes merely by the flick of a line or a dash of colour, but they grin and caper with a startling vitality. His 'Painting 1927' is one of about 115 closely related biomorphic abstractions painted between 1925 and 1927 which constitute collectively the most significant contribution made by any artist to 'automatic' Surrealist painting. A number of forms, white, black, red and yellow, appear against a ground of intense saturated blue which creates a feeling of infinite space. Many of the forms relate to sexual processes at a very elementary level, but they also seem to have been partly inspired by

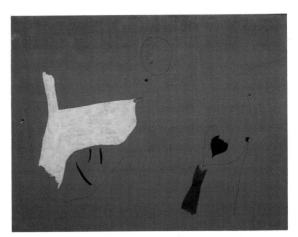

Joan Miró, **Painting** 1927

passages in Apollinaire's play *Les Mamelles de Tirésias* (for Miró was deeply influenced by the Surrealist poets) and perhaps even to be connected with his theme of the circus and the circus horse. His later picture 'Women and Bird in the Moonlight' of 1949 is much more elaborate and highly finished.

Bizarre juxtapositions of images creating a dream-like and sometimes shock effect are found in works as different as Man Ray's 'Pisces', the picture by Pierre Roy and the 'magic' box by Joseph Cornell, while the sculptures by Jean Arp exemplify the overlap with abstract art which occurs at the other extreme of Surrealism. His 'Constellation according to the Laws of Chance' consists of a small number of biomorphic shapes, some painted and some in relief, on a white ground, their arrangement being determined partly by chance, while his free-standing sculpture 'Hybrid Fruit called Pagoda' has a rounded fullness of form which suggests a ripe fruit or parts of the human body.

Jean Arp, **Constellation according to the Laws of Chance** c.1930

British Art 1920–1945

John Nash, **The Cornfield** 1918

Whereas British avant-garde painting of the 1910s was in general an art of emphasis and experiment, as new ideas from abroad were freshly assimilated, the decade from 1920 was calmer, a period of consolidation. Throughout Europe a classical impulse revived. Many British artists had painted monumental compositions relating to the First World War, summarising their stylistic positions of that decade; now, harshness and contrast were less favoured than the renewal of traditional preoccupations with landscape and atmosphere, expressed however through new pictorial idioms.

The work of Paul Nash is rooted in a romantic vision of landscape, a poetic sensitivity to place and a feeling that any form whether natural or man-made can have an inherent personality. These qualities place him in the central stream of the English tradition: it was indeed from a study of landscape and of nineteenth-century mystical painters like Palmer and Rossetti that he confronted the stark and ravaged battlefields of 1917–18 in pictures that established his reputation. The two world wars exactly delimit his mature career; inspired by the second, the anthropomorphic 'Totes Meer' of 1940–1 and his mystical aerial flowers of 1944–6 exemplify the many levelled character of his work, which combines a live continuity of tradition with a restless openness to new currents in art.

Paul Nash's brother John painted many lyrical evocations of the British countryside. Best known is 'The Cornfield', 1918, painted in Buckinghamshire immediately after the First World War when both Paul and John Nash were working on their war paintings, which are now in the Imperial War Museum.

The atmospheric qualities of Paul Nash's art relate closely to similar gentle and introspective preoccupations among artists who came to the fore in the 1920s. David Jones, who worked for a time with Eric Gill, brought a technique of great refinement and precision to visionary designs which are networks of delicate line and formal interplay. In the paintings of Frances Hodgkins, a calculated naïvety of treatment and French-derived tonalities combine with the feeling of weather, mood and place.

There was nothing naïve about Ivon Hitchens, but he used modern French methods, derived from the Fauves and Cubism, for purposes which are traditionally English. Painting almost invariably out of doors, he used resonant colour applied with subtlety in broad gestural brushstrokes responsive to seasonal changes and distance. The landscape is summarised in paint with a wonderful directness and economy; nothing, it seems, is ever touched twice and the freshness of colour and touch becomes a symbol for the perennial freshness of nature.

Ivon Hitchens,
Winter Stage 1936

The naïvety of the primitives has contributed a good deal to the modern understanding of images as objects in themselves. The influence entered British painting through the work of the Cornish fisherman Alfred Wallis, who had just painted 'St Ives' when Christopher Wood and Ben Nicholson discovered him in 1928. However aware of the primitive, Wood was equally alert to the sophisticated innovations of the avant-garde in Paris. Ben Nicholson's early works show the common English sense of place, but he developed a rigour of pictorial structure that is rare, if not unparalleled, in Britain. Nevertheless, his achievement in maturity has often retained a hint of allusive, metaphysical poetry.

Alfred Wallis, **St Ives** *c*.1928

The poetic instinct was stronger in Paul Nash, as 'Voyages of the Moon' demonstrates. Indeed, the poetry of the object on which the Surrealist movement in Paris focused, comes naturally to British art, as painters from the Pre-Raphaelites onward have shown. During the 1930s Nash developed this approach in a series of powerful canvases, which culminated in 'Totes Meer' inspired by a dump of wrecked German aircraft at Cowley, Oxford. In 'Equivalents for the Megaliths', 1935, he mixed the styles of Surrealism and abstraction.

One of the most influential artistic events in London in the 1930s was the International Surrealist Exhibition of 1936, whose organisers included the English Surrealist painter Roland Penrose who was in close contact with many of the Surrealists in Paris. British Surrealism tended however to the representational rather than the automatic variety; a silent unblinking clarity became a strong expressive factor. Examples are Edward Wadsworth's paintings of strongly shaped nautical objects so isolated from their functional processes that they also suggest animal and human roles. 'La Route des Alpes', 1937, by Tristram Hillier was painted in what the artist calls a 'period of transition from abstraction and Surrealism to representational painting', but in the hardness and sharp colour of this picture both formal and emotional qualities remain closely linked. In the work of Edward Burra unease is more immediately apparent: it springs partly from a mood of wry normality in macabre scenes and partly from the nightmarish associations of his figures' bulbous and tapering features. In John Armstrong's work weird imagery is presented in a contemplative, undramatic form. A leading exponent of the opposite approach, exploiting the fantasy inherent in the assembly of previously unrelated objects, was Ceri Richards, whose 'The Female contains all the Qualities', 1937, recalls his larger assemblages. Continental Surrealists had pioneered these procedures; the link is perhaps nowhere clearer than in 'A Symposium', 1936, by Julian Trevelyan which elegantly recalls Miró, yet suggests something of Nicholson's interplay of medium and ground.

Although Cecil Collins exhibited with the Surrealists in 1936 his paintings evoke an inner world and spiritual awakening and the resulting search or quest for a state of paradise or joy.

The strength of British art had lain for several centuries in painting; it was therefore extraordinary that Britain

Paul Nash, **Equivalents for the Megaliths** 1935

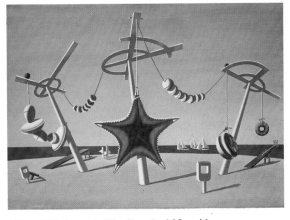

Edward Wadsworth, **The Beached Margin** 1937

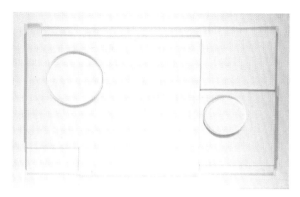

Ben Nicholson, **white relief** 1935

should produce in Henry Moore a sculptor who has become one of the greatest on an international view. Like Barbara Hepworth he was born in Yorkshire and studied art both there and in London. By the end of the 1920s he had established almost all his subsequent themes: the reclining figure, the upright figure, the mother and child, the double head, the mask and the relief.

Moore carved his first near abstract sculpture in 1931, but his liking for multiple readings of a work led him towards Surrealism and away from formal abstraction. He shares with the Surrealists and with Sutherland, for example, the technique of metamorphosis by which

Edward Burra, **Mexican Church** c.1938

several mutually enhancing meanings are given to a single work. The series of reclining figures exemplify this. The figure of 1938 is given the heroic weight and repose of a weathered rock; that of 1939 is worn away to a skeleton, while the bronzes of 1957 and 1960 have the geological scale and age of cliffs, bays and mountains – a deeply telling image of the mother-wife (and the obverse of the cannibalistic relation of mother and baby in the 'Mother and Child' of 1953).

Unlike Hepworth, Moore has never looked to the ideal or for the beautiful in sculpture. His search has been for strength of a different kind. The overall feeling of his sculpture is closer to a sense of the infinite variety of nature than to a sense of underlying order. Or rather the underlying order he observes is the order of flux and the forces of nature expressed through the infinity of human or animal characteristics.

Ceri Richards, **The Female contains all Qualities** 1937

Although a number of British painters had worked under Cubist influence, both before and after the 1914–18 war (see Vorticism) they had all given up painting or had returned to figurative styles in the 1920s. It was not until the thirties that abstract art became firmly rooted here, led by Ben Nicholson and Barbara Hepworth, who early on in the decade had made contact with Brancusi, Arp, Braque, Mondrian and others in Paris. Nicholson turned to abstract art in 1933, and his works of the 1930s include a number of paintings and reliefs executed in a geometrical

Henry Moore
Four-Piece Composition:
Reclining Figure 1934
Cumberland alabaster,
$6\frac{7}{8} \times 18 \times 8$ ($17.5 \times 45.7 \times 20.3$)

In the 1920s and 30s Henry Moore was one of the leaders in a revival of direct carving, finding in the materials part of the subject matter of his work. Thus the grain and organic quality of wood or the toughness of stone became both a source and the integral expression of the forms.

Moore's manipulation of pure form is however his greatest achievement. He has made mass, volume and space a major subject of sculptural investigation. By piercing or dividing masses he encouraged the spectator to explore the spaces between the forms as well as the forms themselves.

Moore regards the human body as the basis of his work. The reclining female figure, partly inspired by an ancient Mexican stone carving of the rain god Chac Mool, has been his principal theme from the 1920s until the present day.

'Four-Piece Composition: Reclining Figure' was one of his most abstract works of the time, and was one of the first in which the human figure is shown dismembered. He has written of this work: 'I am using space in this four-piece reclining figure, in which there is the head part, the leg part, the body and the small round form, which is the umbilicus and which makes a connection'. The incised lines, which counteract the smoothness of the material, only occur on one side of the sculpture; the figure is represented as facing in that direction. The tallest form represents not only the head but the top part of the body including the arms, the declivity also suggests a mouth. The rear or 'boomerang'-shaped element

is a mixture of body and leg, the leg being conceived as resting flat on the ground bent at the knee which is at the very back. The arched upright element represents the other leg, also bent at the knee; its widest part, near the small pebble-like element is the bone of the thigh. The 'pebble' elements is the umbilicus which was important to Moore as a symbol, representing the connection of our life with other life. Moore made the base of the sculpture not rectangular in shape, but irregular, to relate to the positioning of the elements.

The presentation in this sculpture of the human body actually dismembered gives it a strong Surrealist flavour. This is strengthened by the sexual content of the forms and their interrelation, and by the suggestion of orgasmic abandonment. However Moore was never a totally convinced Surrealist. It is his view that in art both the rational and the irrational are present in the creation of a work.

abstract style of great purity. 'white relief', 1935, is painted entirely white and the planes are cut back from the original surface of a mahogany slab, so that the tones are created only by the light that falls on it. 'Painting 1937' is less severe, and has clear luminous colours, but is similarly rectilinear in construction.

Barbara Hepworth was in constant contact in the 1930s with Moore and shared preoccupations with him: the concept of truth to materials, the concern with divided and hollowed-out forms and the poetic allusions to nature. The degree of abstraction and precision of her work connected her equally with Ben Nicholson. Serenity and purity were always important to Hepworth and by the end of the thirties she had established the basis of themes she was to elaborate after the war: the single upright form, the two piece upright forms in echelon, the tall monolith of square upon square, the single and juxtaposed spheres and the hollow sphere.

As a result of the growing threat of war the small band of British abstract artists was reinforced and heartened in the late thirties by the arrival in England of a number of major European artists including Mondrian, Gabo, Moholy-Nagy and the architects Walter Gropius, Mendlesohn and Breuer; for a brief interlude London became a world centre for Constructivist art. However, within a few years all these foreign visitors moved on to the United States, except Gabo who was to follow in 1946.

Shortly before the outbreak of the Second World War Nicholson and Hepworth moved to St Ives in Cornwall, to be joined by Gabo a week or two later and together they formed the nucleus of what was to become the St Ives School.

Most of the totally abstract British art of the 1930s was related to geometrical shapes as in the work of John Piper and Cecil Stephenson. There was also a short-lived interest which evolved out of the art of painting – out of

Sir William Coldstream, **Mrs Winifred Burger** 1936–7

the brushmarks themselves as in Moynihan's series of 'Objective Abstractions' which foreshadowed the Abstract Expressionism of the forties and fifties.

The forms of nature are the most usual theme of Graham Sutherland's work and he belongs to this extent, like Nash and Hitchens, to the tradition of English landscape painting in which nature is used to project the deepest feelings of the painter, but the innovations of the twentieth century have given him the means to add a new poetic dimension. Landscape forms are charged with mystery and drama and sometimes with distinctly erotic overtones, like the roots of an uprooted tree in 'Green Tree Form' which, seen in violent foreshortening, become transformed into a disturbing monster. The powerful, unrealistic colours add to the effect. The pictures which he painted of bombed buildings as an official war artist have a dramatic, tragic quality.

Towards the end of the 1930s, in reaction to the esoteric extremes of abstraction and Surrealism, a number of painters felt it necessary to reaffirm the possibility of 'an unprejudiced approach to the objective world'. They founded in 1937 an art school in London in the Euston Road, with the aim of reviving the figurative tradition of Degas, Cézanne, Bonnard and Sickert. The

Graham Sutherland,
Green Tree Form: Interior of Woods 1940

traditional-sounding programme of William Coldstream and his friends had nevertheless a passion and strength of its own. The preoccupations of these Euston Road painters are shown by the sitters in their portraits here – Coldstream's 'Mrs Burger' reflects the emphasis in the circle around Auden on the specific and the anti-romantic; Gowing's portrait of his charwoman 'Mrs Roberts', the involvement with people in their everyday functions, to which these artists were led by the social problems of the 1930s and by the war. Despite the restrained, tonal styles in which they tended to work, their paintings often have an exceptionally sensitive, lyrical quality – for instance in Graham Bell's 'Dover Front' of 1938 and the early works of Victor Pasmore. Pasmore's 'The Quiet River: The Thames at Chiswick', 1943–4, hints at that development away from representation to which his feeling for abstract form was soon to lead.

L.S. Lowry, **Coming out of School** 1927

an obvious parallel in Surrealism, which coloured much British painting of the 1940s – Sutherland's thorn heads and Moore's shelter sketches are examples. Younger painters like John Minton and John Craxton combined the spirit of Samuel Palmer with the stylistic resources of modern art. Keith Vaughan concentrated increasingly on the figure, as a starting point for near-abstractions in solid but succulent slabs of paint. The Scottish painters Colquhoun and MacBryde gave the style of the forties a tragic mood.

Graham Bell, **Dover Front** 1938

Outside most categories, and working in a style that changed little over forty years, was the Lancashire painter L.S. Lowry; his, at first sight, naïvely simplified treatment of figures in industrial landscapes resulted from long observation and a highly developed sense of pictorial construction. He painted not individuals but communities, and perhaps still more the channels of frozen space between people, linking them together yet holding them apart.

When the Second World War severed contact with Paris, a concern with continuing English qualities and a mood of introspective intensity became common among English painters. This romantic phase was foreshadowed and led by Nash and Sutherland. John Piper abandoned abstraction for strongly lit, richly textured studies of architecture. The recurrent English tendency to see the visible world as embodying an emotional presence had

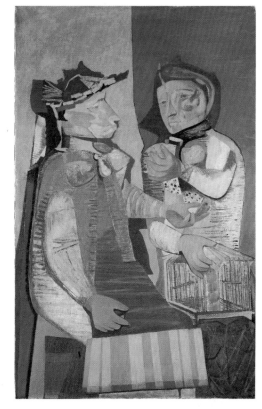

Robert Colquhoun, **The Fortune Teller** 1946

Post-war European Art

Nicolas de Staël, **Marathon** 1948

The devastating effects of the Second World War upon the life and culture of Europe were reflected in its art for well over a decade. The occupation of much of Europe and disruption of cultural activity, the displacement or emigration of many artists from their own countries, the physical and moral toll taken by the war itself, all produced in the short term an uncertainty and lack of direction. The School of Paris in particular, which had for so long dominated Western art, lost this leadership, which passed in the later 1940s to the United States.

In the immediate aftermath of the war, however, the international reputation of Paris and such established masters as Picasso, Matisse or Léger, stood at their height. All these artists went on, in fact, to produce significant new work – for example, Matisse's magnificent *papiers découpés* ('The Snail', 1953), or Léger's large-scale figure compositions which are among their finest achievements.

The fame of these masters inevitably overshadowed the work of their successors. Among the younger generation, a number continued to produce figurative paintings; Gruber, Pignon, and the somewhat younger Bernard Buffet all painted works whose social themes of poverty, isolation or *Angst* earned them the epithet 'Misérabilistes'. The dominant post-war tendency was, however, towards abstraction, with roots in the two contrasting pre-war schools of Cubism and Surrealism. While the works of Poliakoff with their brightly coloured, interlocking planes and to a lesser extent those of Manessier, are Cubist-derived, the majority of painters adopted a much looser, more informal kind of abstraction inspired by the 'organic' Surrealism of artists like Miró, or Masson. This style was known as *art informel* or *tachisme*, after the French word *tache* or brushmark. Among its leading exponents in France were the German-born Hans Hartung who developed an elegant, almost oriental calligraphic style, J.-P. Riopelle, whose intricate play of brushmarks was emphasised by his use of a thick impasto and Pierre Soulages, whose large-scale gestural paintings have been compared with the contemporary works of the American Franz Kline. *Tachisme* did, indeed, have much in common with Abstract Expressionism – both were concerned with fusing gesture and image for example – but whereas the conventions of *belle-peinture* (the concept of a work of art as essentially decorative) tended to inhibit French painters from any radical developments, the best American painting established its superiority by its bold and convincing departures from tradition.

A case in point may be that of Nicolas de Staël, who combined tremendous versatility in the handling of paint with a characteristically French respect for the decorative qualities of a picture. 'Marathon', 1948, is characteristic of de Staël's work before 1951–2. Composed of numerous thickly painted brushmarks, it is related to Riopelle's works, but has a much greater energy, conveying something of the artist's personal struggles at this time. Later de Staël grew dissatisfied with pure abstraction and went on to create, often with a palette knife, attractive works which are in fact highly simplified abstractions from nature – from landscape or still-life motifs. De Staël died young, having achieved a synthesis between his own modernist impulses and the French tradition, but without having broken radically new ground.

This was to be done by the outstanding French artist of his generation, Jean Dubuffet, whose inventiveness over a long working life has influenced many areas of art. The works shown at Dubuffet's first one-man exhibition after the liberation of Paris in 1945 represented a deliberate assault upon *belle-peinture*, upon the conventions of beauty and good taste prevailing in the cultural

Henri Matisse
The Snail 1953
Gouache on cut and pasted paper,
112¾ × 113 (286.5 × 287)

Matisse's paper cut-outs, together with the decoration of the Chapel of the Rosary at Vence, are the crowning achievement of his last years. Unable after 1948 to work at an easel, confined to bed because of ill health, he overcame his difficulties by making a number of paper cut-outs, some of the later ones like this of very large dimensions. He cut out the shapes with a pair of scissors and they were pinned in place by assistants under his direction.

This technique, which he had begun to explore earlier in his picture book *Jazz* and other works, opened up new possibilities for him. 'The paper cut-out', he said, 'allows me to draw in the colour. It is a simplification for me. Instead of drawing the outline and putting the colour inside it – the one modifying the other – I draw straight into the colour'.

'The Snail' was made at the Hôtel Régina at Nice. Matisse always had at his disposal sheets of paper painted in gouache by assistants, in all the colours he used for the cut-outs. A background of white paper – of the dimensions indicated by the artist – was put on the wall and the assistant pinned on to it the pieces of gouached paper, which Matisse passed to him indicating exactly where they should be placed. When later on it was sent to Paris to be pasted down, before anything was moved, an extremely precise tracing was made to ensure that no changes, not even the slightest, were made in the composition.

Its title 'The Snail' comes from the form made up of a succession of patches of colour which curl round like the shell of a snail (and which appear to be caught up in a majestic slow clockwise rotation). The spiral form of a snail's shell echoes the direction of universal movement. Matisse had previously made a number of drawings of snails from nature and the idea for the paper cut-out grew out of these. He became aware of an unrolling and formed an image in his mind purified of the shell.

Made in 1953, the year before his death, 'The Snail' is one of the most abstract of all his works.

Jean Dubuffet, **The Busy Life** 1953

establishment. Convinced that art could only renew it-self from primal, spontaneous sources, Dubuffet turned for inspiration to the crude and direct imagery of Art Brut – graffiti, the art of the insane, of children and of primitive painters.

'Busy Life', 1953, with its graffiti-like figures scratched into the paint clearly evokes such sources, but the picture also gains vitality from the artist's manipulation of the surface, the way he has scratched, rubbed and otherwise enriched the paint. 'Busy Life' has urban associations but in Dubuffet's 'landscapes' a fascination with texture and its power to evoke unexpected images led him to mix

Asger Jorn, **The Timid Proud One** 1957

such ingredients as gravel, earth, sand or extraneous objects such as insects or banana skins into his paint. By such means he could suggest, perhaps, a desert-like landscape in the sandy texture of 'The Exemplary Life of the Soil' – we can see it as a slice of earth tilted upright – or, in other works, the unseen life of the earth pullulating with worms and insects. Dubuffet used common, non-fine art materials to make a wide variety of works – sculptures, 'objects' and 'environments' as well as paint-ings. They serve as starting points for rich imaginative journeys, with metaphysical implications like those of his contemporary, the writer St Exupéry. Dubuffet's later jigsaw-like 'Hourloupe' works which have a flat, undifferentiated paint surface of red, blue and black on white were yet another departure; these elaborate but useless structures evoke a logic of the absurd, and are full of wit and paradox. Dubuffet brought a freshness and intellectual vitality to post-war European art. While much of his work conveys the disenchantment of the period, and has parallels with such existential themes as the alienation and impotence of modern man, or the absurdity of existence, Dubuffet's contribution to post-war art was in the long term a positive, even optimistic one. In his inventive use of 'ordinary' materials and readiness to incorporate into his art both the banal and marvellous aspects of reality, in his attempt to cut across the barriers separating our over-refined culture from the natural world to which we belong, his art proved particu-larly fruitful.

Another assault on 'civilised' values in the post-war period came from the COBRA group in the Netherlands (the participating artists were from COpenhagen, BRussels and Amsterdam) from 1949. Like Dubuffet, these artists found inspiration in crude and primitive imagery, including the art of children, but their violently expressionistic style and preoccupation with myth and symbol were rooted in the Northern tradition of such artists as Munch or Nolde. The Dutchman Karel Appel's paintings, executed in a rich swirling impasto and brilliantly coloured, use a repertory of myth-inspired images, dancing figures, demons or monsters. By contrast the work of the Dane, Asger Jorn, though superficially similar, is quieter and more lyrical, exploiting its fantastic mythological sources ('Timid Proud One', 1957) in a more graphic style .

Dubuffet's fascination with surface texture found a parallel in the work of Antoni Tapies, the outstanding Spanish painter of his generation. 'Grey Ochre' is characteristic of his sober, even sombre canvases whose surfaces are enriched with substances like plaster, sand or dust and inscribed with simple graffiti. Tapies' paintings have an austere beauty which evokes the poor, proud character of Spain herself. Similarly, in the abstract works of Tapies' compatriot Manuel Millares, earth colours, blacks, whites and browns predominate.

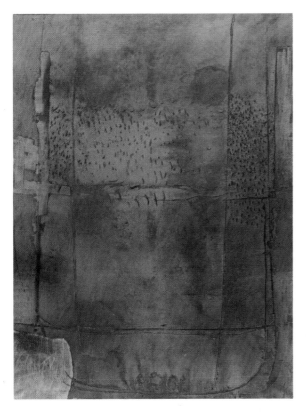

Antoni Tapies, **Grey Ochre** 1958

While abstract forms of art developed rapidly after the war in Italy as elsewhere, a classical traditional strain persisted here. This was due partly to the Fascists' long encouragement of a provincial neo-classicism, partly perhaps to the Italians' more innate conservatism. The classical-Renaissance influence can be seen at its best in the exquisite still lifes of Giorgio Morandi, whose

Giorgio Morandi, **Still Life** 1946

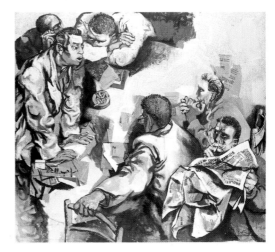

Renato Guttuso, **The Discussion** 1959–60

reputation outside Italy dates from this period. On the other hand, in Italy as elsewhere, opposition to Fascism found expression in works of Social Realism, the foremost exponent of which was Renato Guttuso, a lifelong communist. 'The Discussion' depicts a group of workers engaged in (presumably) ideological debate with a convincing realism.

In the work of Italy's leading post-war abstract painters, Burri and Fontana, the notion of the canvas as a material object on which the artist 'operates' seems uppermost. While Burri, formerly a surgeon, applied roughly cut or torn pieces of sacking, old rags and plastic paints to canvas in a collage-like way, his compatriot Lucio Fontana exploited the surface to contrasting effect. In 'Spatial Concept Pause', 1960, he created, by slashing the bare canvas with a single razor cut, a pictorial 'event' with spatial and emotional associations. A similar fastidious interest in the possibilities of surface texture can be seen in a work by a younger artist, Piero Manzoni, 'Achrome', 1958. Like the Frenchman Yves Klein, Manzoni painted a number of monochrome pictures. Both began from this time to devise a variety of experimental projects which prefigured Conceptual art.

In contrast to the abstract direction taken by avant-garde paintings, the dominant motif of European sculpture for a decade or more after the war was a traditional one – the human figure, which acquired contemporary significance through the imaginative exploitation of materials and the advent of new sculptural techniques. Throughout the 1940s and 1950s, the use of metal was widespread, with bronze casting eventually tending to give way to iron or steel which could be cut or welded.

In Italy, the traditional humanist interest in the human figure and the classical renewal after the war were evident in sculpture. Emilio Greco's nude girls have associations with classical nymphs, for example. But

[115]

other links with traditional Italian culture can be seen in Manzù's bronze 'Cardinal', one of many works on this theme inspired by the sight of seated cardinals at a papal enthronement, and in Marino Marini's 'Horseman', which continues the long tradition of the equestrian statue. Marini, however, reinterpreted the image of the horse and rider in a contemporary way, showing man no longer as a hero but as impotent and afraid. Its sources lay partly in Marini's own experience of war, in the sight of the Lombard peasants fleeing on their frightened horses from the allied bombardment.

Marino Marini, **Horseman** 1947

The outstanding sculptor working in France was Alberto Giacometti, formerly a member of the Surrealist group, whose skeletal bronze figures dating from 1947 are among the most memorable images of post-war European art. These figures represent Giacometti's struggle over many years to express in sculpture what he actually perceived in nature – a deceptively simple aim which involved discarding all the tricks and conventions of academic 'representation' and seeking to realise his vision in all its freshness. In studying the phenomenon of perception, Giacometti observed that people, who can be seen 'whole' only at a distance, appear in relation to the spectator's total field of vision not only comparatively small, but preternaturally elongated and thin, as if compressed by the space that surrounds them; Giacometti's figures (modelled roughly in clay outwards from a metal armature and later cast in bronze) are of several types. While a few walk or point ('Man Pointing', 1949), implying directional movement or relationship with the spectator, most are immobile, hieratic and frontal, like ancient idols; even when set in groups, their relationship is a purely formal one – they remain isolated, closed off, like strangers on the street. A lifelike intensity of gaze – establishing a response to the spectator – characterised Giacometti's late portrait busts and also his painted portraits. In these, space is indicated by a network of lines surrounding the portrait motif.

The impulse behind Giacometti's strange obsessive art was essentially poetic and humanistic; his portrayal of the human figure seems inseparable from the deeply pessimistic mood of the time, and from the images of his contemporaries, which show man as a Camus-like anti-hero, a nervous, fleshless creature imprisoned in an apparently meaningless world. Much of the effect of Giacometti's sculpture lies in its surface texture and the way his bronze surfaces repel, instead of inviting, touch. They also suggest a state of ambivalent meaning, of fluidity. Similar preoccupations underly the disturbing metamorphic bronzes of the Provençal sculptor Germaine Richier. Metamorphosis, or the moment of transformation from one state of being into another, has long been a

Alberto Giacometti, **Man Pointing** 1947

theme of Western art, but unlike Bernini, for example, who could render in classical humanist spirit the metamorphosis of Daphne into a laurel tree, Richier's post-war images of insect- or plant-men or woman-amphora present a bleak image of humankind; the references, underlined by the rough excoriated flesh, to our uncivilised, primal origins and an ever-present sense of decay and death have an obvious contemporary significance. The manipulation of surface underlines the plastic force of César's bat-like 'Man of St Denis', 1958, a part of his 'bestiary'. Its power lies very largely in the rough, evocative texture of the wings made, like the body, by welding together pieces of scrap metal. Just as in painting, the links between texture, our human experience of touch and the world of the imagination were exploited in sculpture. The early bronzes of the Dutchman Carel Visser, and the German Joseph Beuys can also be seen in this context.

The metamorphic idea remained vital throughout the 1950s and beyond, but there was a shift in sensibility,

Eduardo Paolozzi, **Cyclops** 1957

allied to a new awareness of industrial techniques and materials, away from the natural or organic world towards the new world of industrial technology. This gave rise to a rapid development in the sculptural form (pioneered before the war by Picasso and others) of assemblage, involving the assembly of diverse 'found', or non fine-art elements into a single three-dimensional image. The transition is most clearly seen in the early work of Eduardo Paolozzi, who was working in Paris in the late 1940s. 'Cyclops', though moulded and cast in bronze, was in fact made by an assemblage technique. In his later career this artist used spare machine parts and other industrial débris to create a new anthropomorphic image – that of the robot, the junk product of our technological civilisation.

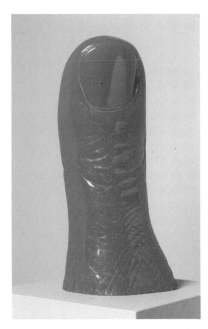

César, **Thumb** 1965

Optical and Kinetic Art

and is relatively little known, the mobiles which the American sculptor Alexander Calder made from the mid 1930s onwards have become immensely popular and have probably been mainly instrumental in establishing kinetic sculpture as a recognised art form. They usually consist of a complex grouping of cut-out metal shapes suspended from thin rods which hang from the ceiling and move freely in the air currents. Noted for their grace, delicacy and wit, they have the appearance of hovering and floating in space. George Rickey is one of those who have been influenced by Calder's example but he has developed his work in a very personal way: his mobiles are always of very simple geometric units usually of stainless steel in a state of delicate balance.

Le Parc's 'Continual Mobile, Continual Light' consists of rows of square mirror plates suspended on threads in front of a white background and lit from the sides by raking lights. Viewed in a darkened space and with the plates set in motion with the aid of electric fans, they create an ever-changing spectacle as moving beams of light are reflected across the back plane or around the room itself, and mingle with the play of cast shadows. The Gallery's work by Gerhard von Graevenitz comprises simply five vertical black panels mounted in front of a square white back plane, but they are made to move slowly sideways, converging or diverging in a manner

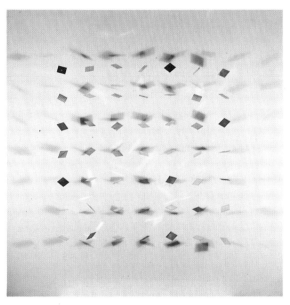

Julio Le Parc, **Continual Mobile, Continual Light** 1963

Among the new types of abstract art which have become prominent since the Second World War (though with origins going back earlier) are Optical and Kinetic Art. The former is concerned with the exploration of perception and visual phenomena such as moiré effects, after-images and so on, and the latter with the introduction of actual movement. There is sometimes an overlap between the two, and both tend to have something of the character of scientific experiments, of a systematic exploration of new techniques and materials. It is not for nothing that one of the groups of artists working on these and related lines – a group formed in Paris in 1960 which included Yvaral, Morellet, Le Parc and Sobrino – took the name Groupe de Recherche d'Art Visuel.

The Tate is fortunate to possess what is probably the very first true kinetic sculpture, the 'Vibrating Form' made by Naum Gabo in Moscow in 1919–20 which consists of a thin metal rod mounted on a motor which causes it to vibrate from side to side and create the illusion of a standing wave.

Whereas this was an isolated work in Gabo's oeuvre

Pol Bury, **16 Balls, 16 Cubes in 8 Rows** 1966

Josef Albers, **Study for 'Homage to the Square: Departing in Yellow'** 1964

who painted an extensive series of pictures from 1949 onwards entitled 'Homage to the Square' in which he used a standardised geometrical composition as the framework for a study of colour relationships. The compositional schema in its complete form, consisting of three squares within a square, can be seen in 'Homage to the Square: Departing in Yellow', but in many of the other pictures one or other of the three inner squares is omitted in order to increase the area of particular colour. Despite these self-imposed limitations, Albers achieved an extraordinary variety of colour effects: receding and advancing colours, expanding and contracting colour areas, positive areas and negative areas, and so on.

Victor Vasarely, **Supernovae** 1959–61

which suggests that the space is being squeezed or stretched. Both these works are random in their movements and avoid one of the frequent limitations of this kind of art, namely a tendency for the works to go through an exact cycle which is endlessly repeated.

Whereas most Kinetic Art stems from the Constructivist tradition, both Pol Bury and Harry Kramer have made kinetic works which have a more Surrealist character and are often full of surprises and humour. Bury, who began as a Surrealist painter, has concentrated since the late 1950s on making sculptures which move with a jerky, almost hypnotic slowness. One watches the unfolding of a mini-drama as his wooden balls and cubes edge sideways or struggle to heave themselves upwards in defiance of the laws of gravity, while his so-called 'tactile vibrations' consist of clusters of thin filaments projecting from a flat ground which twitch and move in a random, unpredictable way. Kramer's delicate cage-like wire sculptures shaped like a torso or a sledge have a complicated internal system of wheels and elastic with all the mad complexity of a Heath Robinson machine.

As has already been noted, certain features anticipating Op Art can be found in such earlier works as the Léger 'Still Life with a Beer Mug' of 1921–2 (vibrant, aggressively contrasting black-and-white patterns) and the Tate's Mondrian of c.1937–42 (a dazzle effect at the points where the black lines intersect), but it was only in the late 1940s and 1950s that artists began to take optical phenomena like these as their principal theme for investigation. One of the first artists to work systematically along these lines was the Bauhaus-trained Josef Albers,

Vasarely is usually regarded as the leader of Optical Art and the Gallery's three works by him show different phases of his development. All are concerned with the exploration of visual effects. 'Nives II' stems from the tradition of French geometrical abstraction except that there are certain deliberate ambiguities of perspective which cause the eye to see the forms sometimes behind and sometimes in front of one another. 'Supernovae' is based on a grid of squares, some of which have been altered or replaced with circles according to simple rules. It is painted in the maximum contrast of black and white, with the dazzling effect of a series of explosions (supernovae = star explosions). Finally, 'Banya' is composed entirely of a simple figure – a rhombus in a square – repeated over and over again, and conveys an effect of glowing colour and flickering movement. Bridget Riley produces a rather similar effect in 'Fall' by means of undulating black and white lines which appear to oscillate and shift disturbingly before one's eyes. The dynamic pattern and strong contrasts make a violent assault upon the retina. 'Deny II', with its variations in the orientation and tone of the small lozenge shapes, has a gentle flowing movement. In her more recent pictures, such as 'Late Morning', she has begun to use bands of pure colour which tint the white lines adjacent to them.

Various other artists have worked with superimposed forms which appear to vibrate or dissolve or change their configuration through the movement of the spectator (unlike true kinetic works which have their own built-in movement). Soto, one of the most distinguished of them, uses a simple technique in 'Cardinal' and 'Relationships of Contrasting Elements'. Rods or squares are placed a few inches in front of a grid of parallel black and white lines so that as they or one's eyes move a flickering effect is produced. This seems to dematerialise the forms and to turn them into a complex of patches of light in deep space, and thus he can give a far greater richness to the liturgical solemnity of his forms and colours. A similar moiré technique is used by Yvaral (the son of Vasarely) in his 'Kinetic Relief – Optical Acceleration', while the Swede Eric Olson and the Spaniard Francisco Sobrino have both made objects which change markedly in appearance when viewed from different angles. The relief by Cruz-Diez, with its row of vertical struts, is constructed in such a way that the colours appear to change completely as one walks past it from one side to the other.

Bridget Riley, **Deny II** 1967

Abstract Expressionism and Post-painterly Abstraction in the USA

In a number of ways the paintings of the New York School after about 1950 look radically different from any produced in Europe earlier this century. Most obvious is their greatly enlarged scale, often closer to mural than easel painting, the canvas tending to fill the spectator's field of vision. Closely connected with this is the impact of such works. In much post-war American painting colour and/or brushstrokes are boldly simplified and intensified for maximum effect. Thirdly, there is a new emphasis on the painted surface, an 'all-over' look, in which lateral expansion – i.e. towards the edges of the canvas – replaces the traditional European concern with composition in depth, and fourthly, as part of this interest in surface, one finds a strong emphasis on the process of painting itself and the physical properties of the medium.

Behind the emergence of such paintings lay the search for a style at once American and contemporary, whose roots lay in the Depression years of the 1930s. During this decade, several factors brought American art out of its comparative provincialism and isolation; the Federal Art Project of 1935–43 set up under Roosevelt's New Deal, employed large numbers of artists on public projects such as mural painting, and the decoration of public buildings. From operating, as they had done previously in a cultural vacuum and without support, many artists who emerged after the war as leading Abstract Expressionists (including Pollock, Rothko, Gorky and Baziotes) gained from the Project a vital experience of professional status, of social engagement and, perhaps most important of all, of artistic community. Most of the art produced by the Project was figurative, tending to Social Realism, but through their association the younger artists became aware of, and increasingly interested in, developments in European abstraction; this was fuelled not only by art magazines and books but by the formation and growth of the great American public collections (e.g. the Museum of Modern Art in New York, founded 1929), which institutions also mounted major exhibitions of contemporary European art. As a result, the Americans could study at first hand the work of such artists as Picasso, Kandinsky or Miró and assess movements like Cubism or Surrealism for themselves. Much activity in the later 1930s centred on New York, where groups of artists interested in contemporary trends (e.g. the American Abstract Artists, or The Ten) met to discuss and exhibit their work, and where the German abstract painter Hans Hofmann held his influential studio-school. Finally, as the certainty of war approached, large numbers of European artists arrived in New York as refugees; these included not only most of the leading Surrealists (among them André Breton, Max Ernst, Yves Tanguy, Salvador Dali and Matta) but also such major figures as Piet Mondrian and Fernand Léger. The work of these artists was now made available additionally through the New York dealers, and personal contacts were established in some cases. The stimulus of these events undoubtedly underlies the emergence of a native abstract school after the war, but Abstract Expressionism (the name was originally coined to describe Kandinsky's art) came to involve a slow but deliberate repudiation of European models (and culture). Paradoxically, underlying the emergence of the new abstraction was a sense of crisis in the existing content of art, which was intensified by the advent of world war. On the one hand, Social Realism, tied as it was to the ideology of the Left, now seemed discredited. On the other, many younger American artists saw the aesthetics of post-Cubist abstraction as decorative and sterile, empty of meaning. In a letter to the *New York Times* of

Arshile Gorky, **Waterfall** 1943

June 1943, Mark Rothko, Adolph Gottlieb and Barnett Newman posited loftier aims for their own art: 'There is no such thing as painting about nothing ... we assert that the subject is crucial and only that subject matter is valid which is tragic and timeless.' The same letter paid tribute to the liberating philosophy of Surrealism, yet clearly implied that art must now go beyond the illustration of dreams and find its source within the individual, or 'felt' experience of each artist.

The first generation of Abstract Expressionists drew, in fact, much inspiration from the techniques if not the content of Surrealism – particularly from the organic abstractions of artists like Miró, Masson and the Chilean, Matta. Arshile Gorky, who exhibited with the Surrealists-in-Exile, provides a link between the European Surrealist and Expressionist traditions and the distinctively American abstraction of his younger contemporary Jackson Pollock. Initially influenced by Picasso and Miró, 'Waterfall' exemplifies Gorky's mature style with its fluid open handling (the paint has been allowed to trickle down the canvas), its vocabulary of unspecific, but highly suggestive biomorphic shapes and its mood of poetic reverie, much admired by his contemporaries. Nevertheless, as in this work (which originated in studies of a country waterfall) Gorky always retained in his canvases elements of external nature – which those who came after him sought to eliminate.

Jackson Pollock, **Yellow Islands** 1952

Like Gorky, Pollock experimented with the Surrealist technique of 'automatism' or spontaneous drawing as a way of liberating the creative energies of the unconscious mind. Through his mastery of this technique Pollock's works (previously figurative and expressionistic) became progressively more abstract and free until in his drip paintings of 1947 he achieved an art of pure gestural abstraction. Some of Pollock's works were made by dripping paint from a brush or stick on to a canvas placed

flat on the floor, the rhythmical movements of the painter's arm creating an intricate pattern of lines over the surface; this technique, though highly improvisatory, nevertheless allowed the artist a high degree of control over the finished picture. In 'Yellow Islands', 1952, Pollock incorporated a greater element of 'chance' through pouring and staining, and then standing the canvas upright and adding some further black paint which was left to trickle down the surface.

In Pollock's wake, the idea of the canvas as a field for action, of painting as a record of the artist's own creative processes, became widely accepted towards the end of the decade. Spontaneity and 'risk' in art acquired an absolute value – a romantic and individualistic view which was probably also fostered by the post-war climate of Existentialism.

The artist's struggles, passions, hesitations are all apparent in the canvases of the Dutch-born painter Willem de Kooning. Like Pollock, de Kooning was a genuine Expressionist but chose to work in a more conventional way with oil, brushes and canvas. 'The Visit', painted over several months and subject to frequent changes of mind characteristically combines voluptuousness and savagery, voluptuousness in the choice and handling of pigment, savagery in the violent distortion to which de Kooning subjects the female figure – always a central theme of his art. More abstract and meditative in character is a canvas like 'The Return' by Philip Guston, where a similar process of tentative application, of vision and revision in clusters of ribbon-like brushstrokes reveal the artist's struggle to achieve complete self-expression. Among the gestural painters, many of whose works derive from the organic abstractions of Miró, the use of 'biomorphic' imagery was prevalent. Baziotes' 'Mammoth', for instance, evokes the life of primitive organisms suspended in a mysterious underwater world, and has a quiescent, dreamlike quality.

More typical of the kind of art we associate with the gestural type of Abstract Expressionism, indeed gestural painting writ large, are the canvases of Franz Kline, a friend and admirer of de Kooning. Kline's characteristically bold and uncompromising works often set black 'gesture' against white canvas to create a dramatic and formal tension. Kline's imagery, although abstract, evokes the architecture of the modern city reminding us (perhaps unintentionally) of such massive structures as girders, bridges or skyscrapers.

An alternative, and ultimately more influential mode of Abstract Expressionism was developed by the so-called Colour Field painters after 1947. Its chief exponents, Mark Rothko, Barnett Newman and Clyfford Still, who had all earlier used automatic procedures and drawn on Jungian myth and symbol in their works, now began to find in the exploration of colour, rather than gesture, their ideal expressive mode. These artists

Mark Rothko
Black on Maroon 1958
Oil on canvas,
105 × 144 (266.7 × 365.8)

This canvas is one of nine now in
the Tate Gallery which Rothko
originally painted to decorate the
Four Seasons Restaurant in the
Seagram Building, New York. At the
time the project was initiated (by,
among others, Philip Johnson who
with Mies van der Rohe was co-
architect of the skyscraper), Rothko
was internationally recognised as one
of the leading Colour Field painters of
the Abstract Expressionist School.
Given a free hand to design the wall
decorations as he wished, Rothko
worked on the commission in his
New York studio for eight months
during 1958–9, producing in all
three different series of canvases. At

the end of this period he decided to
withhold them, on the grounds that
they were unsuitable for such a
luxurious and worldly setting.

Mark Rothko's characteristically
large abstract canvases, in which
softly painted rectangular planes of
luminous colour seem to 'float' or
hover in front of a coloured ground,
date from around 1950. In the earlier
works of this type, he tended to use
rich, vibrant colour harmonies, but
in the latter part of his career his
works became increasingly sombre
and tragic in feeling. In the
'Seagram' series he deliberately
sought a brooding, claustrophobic
effect, like that achieved by
Michelangelo in the blank windows
of the Laurentian Library at
Florence, which he much admired.

Like those of Barnett Newman
and Clyfford Still, Rothko's works
were visionary in their aims.

Through their very large scale,
which dominates the spectator's field
of vision, the artist seeks to draw him
'into' the painting, which becomes
an object of contemplation. It is not
inappropriate to see the floating
rectangles as so many 'doors' or
'windows' on to a transcendental
reality.

When Rothko decided in 1969 to
present these canvases to the Tate
Gallery (one factor was the knowledge that they would hang in the
same building as the works of
J.M.W. Turner), he stipulated that,
as originally conceived, they should
create a complete environment and
hang in their own enclosed space. He
worked out in his studio the exact
sequence in which they should be
placed and looked forward to seeing
them installed here. By a sad irony,
they arrived in England on the day of
his death, in 1970.

Clyfford Still, **1953** 1953

compositions in which large expanses of saturated colour are bound by jagged or flame-like contours often bear this out. '1953' is a characteristic example of Still's approach.

Barnett Newman carried the colour field idea to more extreme limits than his contemporaries, and was the most influential of the three. The Tate's two pictures, 'Eve' 1950 and 'Adam' 1951–2, are typical of his large scale abstractions with their single undifferentiated layers of colours activated by one or more narrow vertical bands or zips of contrasting colour. Newman deliberately avoided the conspicuous brushwork of his contemporaries and sought an impersonal, even austere look in keeping with his aspiration to universality. Having started to paint fluently again after an interruption of some five years, and trying to make a fresh start and re-think painting again from the beginning, he tended to choose titles relating to the act of creation ('The Beginning', 'Genetic Moment'), Old Testament

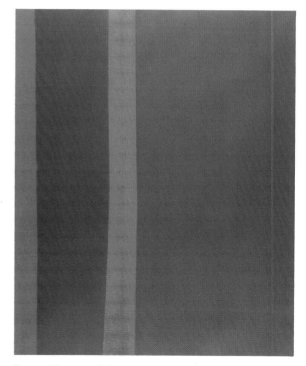

Barnett Newman, **Adam** 1951–2

became dedicated to the purest, most uncompromising abstraction, relying for their effect upon the expressive power of colour and the division of the field. From about 1950 their canvases became increasingly large 'fields' of colour, with a characteristically simplified and unified paint surface. Like Monet's late water-lily paintings they were intended to function as murals, to be seen close to and to surround and draw-in the spectator. Behind this art lay visionary aspirations, articulated cogently by Barnett Newman, the chief theorist of the style, in numerous articles from the late 1940s. Influenced by Burke's notion of the Sublime, Newman predicated a metaphysical art going beyond conventional notions of the beautiful and communicating with the spectator at a transcendental level. The strength and conviction of the best Colour Field painting does, in fact, derive from this metaphysical basis.

Rothko was probably the most seductive, or sensuous, of the Colour Field painters. His large, luminous canvases whose central planes appear to hover in front of a coloured ground seem to invite the spectators to immerse themselves in contemplation. Less immediately appealing perhaps, but also powerful, are the works of Clyfford Still whose stark and raw paint surfaces represent his deliberate repudiation of 'the beautiful' in favour of a more universal truth. Still wanted to create visual metaphors for the sublime, and the vertical drift of his

prophets ('Abraham') and so on. 'Adam' and 'Eve' as the first man and first woman were in keeping with this.

Even as Abstract Expressionism was becoming internationally recognised in the early 1950s as the leading post-war movement in art (it was vigorously promoted abroad, partly as a manifestation of American democracy in the Cold War era) a reaction to it set in at home. Many artists objected to the rhetorical and sensuous excesses of

Morris Louis, **Alpha-Phi** 1961

the gestural school, the movement's cult of individualism and the 'confessional' overtones of many works. Ad Reinhardt, for example, whose work has been closely associated with that of Newman and Rothko, publicly adopted a purist 'art for art's sake' position, his own canvases showing a progressively cool, reductivist approach which led him to eliminate more and more, and to work exclusively in monochrome, first in red or blue, and finally in near black, with a mysterious matt surface and a barely discernible cruciform design. The shift away from Abstract Expressionism towards what the critic Clement Greenberg later termed 'post-painterly' or hard-edged abstraction was part of a widespread change of mood in the 1960s, a lifting of the *angst*-ridden post-war climate everywhere. It can be clearly seen in the work of two Washington painters, Morris Louis and Kenneth Noland. Between 1957 and 1962, when he died, Louis moved from his loose, sensuously painted, 'Veil' paintings (made by staining unsized canvas with layers of liquid acrylic paint) towards tauter, more formalised canvases employing regular parallel stripes of pure colour. A work like 'Alpha Phi', 1961, is transitional between the two.

Like Ad Reinhardt's, Kenneth Noland's works had their roots in the geometric art of the 1920s and 1930s, and here an important influence was that of his teacher, the veteran Josef Albers, who had formerly taught at the Bauhaus. Albers' art consisted in the systematic exploration of colour relationships within a standardised geometric framework, in his case typically the square. In the late 1950s Noland adopted a similar approach in 'target' pictures like 'Gift' in which concentric circles are painted according to a premeditated scheme. The appeal of Noland's chromatic paintings seems no longer emotional, but primarily intellectual and optical. He exercised, in comparison with, say, Pollock, a high degree of control over the image, by adapting his means to the flat picture surface and substituting for oil a thinned acrylic paint

with a matt surface, staining the canvas and reducing the hand-crafted look. The development of this reductive but strongly coloured abstract style during the 1960s owes much to the influence of art critics like Greenberg, in whose eyes 'modernist' aesthetic painting was seen as a matter of respecting 'essentials' – i.e. the flatness of the pictorial surface and the shape of its support.

Among the most original exponents of hard-edged abstraction was Ellsworth Kelly, whose works are marked by a similarly high degree of intellectual control and an impeccably 'cool' or impersonal finish. Kelly, who worked in Paris in the early 1950s, was particularly influenced by the shapes and colours in Matisse's late paper cut-outs and a similar boldness and vitalism pervades his own paintings. He was a pioneer of the

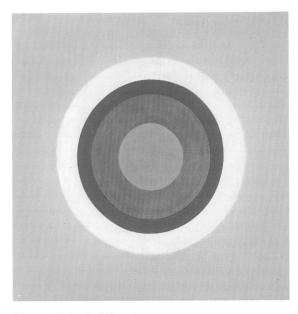

Kenneth Noland, **Gift** 1961-2

David Smith, **Cubi XIX** 1964

The dynamism of Smith's works, together with their scale and impact, have much in common with the contemporary work of the Abstract Expressionist painters.

shaped canvas and of the tendency, widespread in the 1960s, to fuse the essential elements of a picture, its colour, surface and shape, into a single abstract form.

In the work of Frank Stella the hard-edged school found what was probably its most complete expression. The principles underlying it led on to the Minimal art of the later 1960s.

Among the distinguished American sculptors of this period are Louise Nevelson and David Smith. Nevelson achieved fame in the later 1950s with her 'walls' of wooden boxes painted a uniform black, white or gold. These intricate structures – of which the Tate has two – assemble within their compartments a wide diversity of elements, including 'found' objects such as rolling pins or sections of banisters, as well as hand-carved forms.

More influential, particularly on the next generation of sculptors, were David Smith's welded iron and steel sculptures of the 1950s and early 1960s. While some of his earlier works were figurative, influenced by the iron constructions made by Picasso and Gonzalez in the 1930s, later works like 'Cubi XIX' are purely abstract. This is one of a series of twenty-eight monumental works in stainless steel, consisting of simple, geometric elements piled one above another in a state of precarious balance.

British Post-war Art from 1945–60

The end of the war brought a renewal of contacts with Europe, and particularly with the School of Paris. Exhibitions of Picasso and Matisse, of Rouault, Braque and Klee were held in London immediately after the war, and conversely, the work of artists like Henry Moore and Ben Nicholson was shown abroad, establishing their international reputation. Exhibitions apart, there was a rapid growth in art books and periodicals, and British artists were once again free to travel abroad. Despite these contacts, the war had generated a mood of caution and introspection, a disinclination for formal experiment and a preoccupation with purely British concerns, which made art here look conservative by continental standards. It was not until the mid 1950s that British painting – in marked contrast to its vitality in the later 1930s – again contributed to the European mainstream.

This was partly because the war had dispersed many artists from the capital. The art which could be seen in London in the 1940s and early 1950s was largely dominated by the figurative realism of the Euston Road painters and their associates who continued to make straight no-nonsense portraits, still lifes and landscapes, or to paint nudes in a studio setting. Similarly the work coming out of the Royal College of Art or Royal Academy Schools remained largely traditional, tending increasingly to an unvarnished realism and a pre-occupation with ordinary urban subject matter. Rodrigo Moynihan's 'Group Portrait' of the teaching staff at the R.C.A. painted for the Festival of Britain in 1951 seems particularly evocative, not only of the prevailing style, but of the atmosphere and leading figures of the period. It includes Moynihan himself, John Minton, Carel Weight and Ruskin Spear among others.

The most significant developments came from artists associated with neo-Romanticism, among whom a handful gave expression to the spiritual desolation of war. Graham Sutherland's 'Crucifixion', 1946, reflects both his despair and his renewal of religious faith at this time. The distorted limbs and features of Christ were inspired not only by such prototypes as Grünewald's Isenheim Altarpiece, but by the immediate horror of photographs of Auschwitz and Buchenwald.

The portraits Sutherland made after the war reflect, in part, the renewed interest in realism. The earliest of these, and probably the most famous, is the Somerset Maugham of 1949, in which the novelist emerges as some not-altogether-likeable oriental sage. His features, treated by Sutherland in an almost topographical way, recall the gnarled roots and stumps of his Welsh landscapes. From the 1950s, further elements of unease enter Sutherland's work, for example in a number of paintings featuring thorny or spiky forms, cactus-like presences which seem to be presaged in the row of spiky ferns hanging above Maugham's head and by the non-naturalistic heightening of his colours.

Although Sutherland remained essentially a landscape painter, his work has parallels with that of two younger artists, Francis Bacon and Lucian Freud, who have concentrated almost exclusively on the human figure. Francis Bacon's 'Three Studies for Figures at the base of

Francis Bacon, **Three Studies for Figures at the base of a Crucifixion** 1944

a Crucifixion' was in fact shown alongside works by Sutherland in 1945, but the passion and ferocity of Bacon's vision, in which the traditional trio of mourners become the screaming furies of Greek tragedy, announced something new in British art. The vision of man as tortured and humiliated, isolated in a private hell, has been the constant theme of Bacon's art, shown in images which have ranged from figures crouching beside hunks of raw meat to the many intimate portraits he has made of his friends.

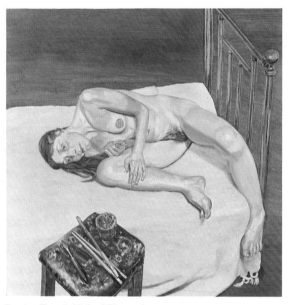

Lucian Freud, **Naked Portrait** 1972–3

Lucian Freud, himself the subject of several of Bacon's portraits, spent his early childhood in the Berlin of the 1920s, and many of his own portraits carry more than a hint of German *Neue Sachlichkeit* in their obsessive, hypnotic realism. Unlike Bacon's, Freud's early portraits of friends in interior settings are detached and deadpan, conveying a contemporary sense of unease through their atmosphere of tension and their brooding, introspective quality, as in 'Girl with White Dog', 1950–1. In later works Freud has adopted a looser more painterly style, emphasising the quality of the sitter's flesh as much as his psychology; 'Naked Portrait', 1972, is one of a recent masterly series of nudes.

Urban landscape has played an important part in the work of Leon Kossoff and Frank Auerbach, both pupils in the early 1950s of the veteran landscapist and former Vorticist-associate David Bomberg. While Bomberg's own most impressive post-war works are probably his strong, highly coloured West Country landscapes painted in the summers of 1946–7 ('Tregor and Tregoff, Cornwall'), the younger artists have sought landscape motifs close to home, ones with which they are very familiar. Kossoff's 'Demolition of the Old House, Dalston Junction', and Auerbach's studies of Primrose Hill or an Oxford Street Building Site are characteristic of their approach. Both artists paint very quickly but tend to destroy and rebuild the image many times before achieving the rawness, individuality and highly charged end result that they are seeking. Auerbach's heavily impasted works (which also include an important series of nudes) are built up of thick paint applied very often in slashing brushstrokes which create a vigorous interaction of forms and masses.

The Welfare State mood of the 1950s and the advent of a self-consciously working class culture (epitomised by the early novels of Kingsley Amis and Alan Sillitoe, or the plays of Osborne and Wesker) was echoed in the familiar, unglamorous subject matter of the so-called Kitchen Sink painters, who achieved great popular success between 1953 and 1956. John Bratby, Jack Smith, Edward Middleditch and Derrick Greaves, all students at the Royal College of Art at the time of Moynihan's group portrait, 1951, seem, however, to have painted their families and immediate surroundings more because of their own impoverished circumstances than out of any socially conscious motive. Bratby was the most expressionistic of the four. His contemporary 'Still Life with a Chip Frier' combines realism of subject (the

Jack Smith, **Mother bathing Child** 1953

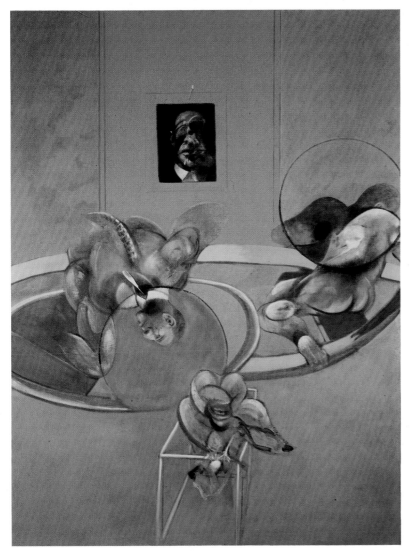

does not, for example, require the sitter's presence. They are, rather, paintings which express a wider truth about the subject's life and relationship to the artist, in the context of Bacon's own anguished view of the human situation.

In this picture, for example, the two main figures, and possibly also the 'portrait' on the wall, all render aspects of a single person, the artist's close friend George Dyer who had died four years earlier but who was none the less 'present' for Bacon in 1975.

The wider implications of such paintings are revealed, not only by Bacon's formal innovations, but by his use of a limited range of supporting images or 'props', drawn from a variety of cultural sources. For example, the owl-like figure with a screaming head in the foreground of this work fuses a traditional symbolic image of sleep or death (the owl), or possibly the Furies, with Bacon's longstanding preoccupation with the human scream inspired by such images as the screaming woman in Einstein's *The Battleship Potemkin*; the isolation of the spine in the left-hand figure, and the transparent and circular treatment of the figures overall seem indebted to Bacon's longstanding interest in radiographs or medical x-ray photographs.

Bacon has been called an artist in the grand manner and he is certainly one of the great virtuoso painters of our time. By adopting (with ingenious departures) a traditional post-Renaissance format in his works – i.e. by setting his figures plastically within a measurable illusionistic space – he creates an intimate pictorial theatre. Through this device the spectator is made a voyeur, sharing complicity in the shocking or disturbing scene he witnesses.

Francis Bacon
Three Figures and Portrait 1975
Oil and pastel on canvas,
78 × 58 (198.1 × 147.3)

Francis Bacon is one of the twentieth century's great portraitists, but of a highly unconventional kind. For over thirty years he has been making intimate portraits of his friends, whom he depicts in a variety of distorted or anguished poses within the setting of a confined interior space. Such works are not of course 'objective', in any accepted sense – Bacon

objects assembled on the table came from his kitchen) with a sophisticated awareness of the techniques of predecessors such as Bonnard, in the high viewpoint and tilted table-top. Jack Smith's 'Mother bathing Child', 1953, seems less self-conscious, being treated with a tender but unvarnished realism. These artists, like the Polish painter Josef Herman, who made a series of studies of Welsh miners at this period, found a vigorous champion in the Marxist critic John Berger.

In 1952, a number of younger British sculptors (Adams, Armitage, Butler, Chadwick, Clarke, Meadows, Paolozzi and Turnbull) made a particularly strong contribution to the Venice Biennale. Their work included both bronze casts and forged iron constructions, and the most *Angst*-ridden images were referred to by Herbert Read as expressing the 'Geometry of Fear'. Reg Butler made forged and welded iron figures between 1948 and 1951 and then changed to making modelled human figures on still prominent armatures. Lynn Chadwick was making skeleton-like constructions and the half-animal, half-human figures, modelled with metal composition on iron frameworks, that have characterised his work.

While figurative art largely dominated the London art scene after the war, developments which would bring British art back into the forefront of European abstraction were taking place outside London, notably at St Ives where Ben Nicholson and Barbara Hepworth had settled in 1939. It was here that the traditions of European Constructivism explored by both artists in the 1930s became merged with a peculiarly English lyrical and sensuous response to nature. In curved and stringed wood carvings like 'Pelagos', 1946, whose interior is painted pale blue, Barbara Hepworth tried to express a

Dame Barbara Hepworth, **Pelagos** 1946

Victor Pasmore,
Square Motif, Blue and Gold: The Eclipse 1950

sense of identification with nature: 'Every sculpture contains to a greater or lesser degree the ever-changing contours, embodying my own response to the landscape. The colour in the concavities plunged me into the depth of water, caves or shadows . . . the strings were the tension I felt between myself and the sea, the wind and the hills.' Later works evoke through their upright forms the human presence or monoliths in the landscapes, or in pierced oval or spherical forms, the idea of enclosure or embrace suggested by the contours of nature. Many of Hepworth's works from the 1950s, when she abandoned carving for a time, were cast in bronze or other metals and, partly in response to public commissions, grew more monumental in size. In the last years of her life she returned to carving and to the more geometric and formal style of the 1930s.

In Ben Nicholson's post-war work, landscape, still life and relief were increasingly fused into abstract works redolent of the light, textures and colours of Cornwall. At first he incorporated recognisable still-life elements like mugs or jars into his landscapes. Later, in works like 'Vertical Seconds', 1953, the shapes of such objects took on a more abstract function, creating a rhythmical interplay of overlapping linear silhouettes, alternating with planes of pure colour and areas of semi-transparent texture. In the large carved and painted reliefs of the 1960s such as 'Ice-off blue', Nicholson returned to a central theme of the 1930s, the white paint and geometric treatment of that period now giving way to a freer, more majestic style. Though abstract, Nicholson's later reliefs incorporate the colours and textures of nature – silvery whites, umbers and greys, a roughness of rocks and stones – evoking the places that inspired them.

The two contrasting aspects of Nicholson's work – Constructivism and nature-abstraction – were taken up and developed separately by the two emerging abstract schools of the 1950s. The most influential figure in the former group was Victor Pasmore, a co-founder of the Euston Road School and painter of a number of poetic and evocative landscapes in the early 1940s, whose 'conversion' to abstraction seems to have occurred quite independently of any outside influence in 1948. By 1950 he was producing abstract compositions like 'Square Motif, Blue and Gold: the Eclipse', in which organic shapes alternate with such strictly geometric motifs as the square, circle or triangle. In that year, Pasmore made contact with Nicholson in St Ives, joined the newly formed Penwith Society of Artists and began regular visits to the West Country. Despite the classical bias he shared with Nicholson, however, the strongly theoretical basis of Pasmore's abstraction (which became through a series of collage and relief constructions increasingly 'pure' and severe) distinguished him and his followers from the St Ives artists. Pasmore's circle in the early 1950s included Kenneth and Mary Martin and Anthony Hill, who work in two and three dimensions, and the painters Adrian Heath and Terry Frost. Kenneth Martin has continued to work in the Constructivist idiom, making a wide range of works including series of paintings such as the 'Chance and Order' series, which are based on a set of predetermined rules that include an element of chance.

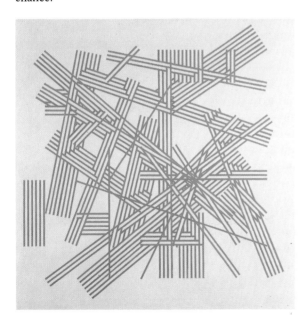

Kenneth Martin,
Chance and Order 10 (Monastral Blue) 1972

An alternative direction drawing its inspiration from the organic shapes of nature was developed by a younger generation of artists, many of whom settled in or were frequent visitors to West Cornwall. The only Cornish-born artist of this group, Peter Lanyon, also expressed what was, perhaps, the most deeply felt response to nature. A pupil of Nicholson and Naum Gabo in the early 1940s, his early works like 'Porthleven', 1951, the Cornish port of that name, reflect the Constructive approach of these older artists; it was in fact painted with the help of three-dimensional models as a way of establishing the position of forms in space. Later Lanyon developed a much freer and more painterly style, giving lyrical expression to his feeling for nature and the elements. 'Thermal', 1960, was inspired by the experience of gliding and conveys the sensation of passing through air with the currents rising about him.

Peter Lanyon, **Porthleven** 1951

Other St Ives artists who combined, in very different ways, Nicholson's Constructivist approach with a personal response to landscape include John Wells, Bryan Wynter and Wilhelmina Barns-Graham. Terry Frost, who has spent much of his life working in West Cornwall, has been influenced not only by that countryside but by the open spaces of Yorkshire where he spent three years in the mid-1950s.

In the work of Roger Hilton and William Scott after 1950, the influence of European art began to make itself newly felt, but in a completely assimilated form. In Hilton's early abstract 'Painting', 1953, some influence of Mondrian can be seen in the simple division of the surface into a few irregular compartments painted in primary white, red and black; if the motif is derivative, however, Hilton's handling of paint and colour are entirely personal. His later works, whether abstractions suggested by the forms of nature or figure compositions like 'Oi Yoi Yoi', 1963, are remarkable for their freshness, varied handling of texture and the expressiveness of their scribbled calligraphic lines. Similarly, the early influence of such French painters as Bonnard and Nicolas de Staël became thoroughly assimilated into Scott's abstract works after 1951. 'Ochre Painting', 1958, derives its shapes from ordinary household objects such as saucepans on a kitchen table, but the sophisticated way these shapes, colours and textures are welded into a unified whole is Scott's own.

After 1956, the European influence was replaced by that of New York. Although a number of British artists had visited America in the earlier 1950s, and been greatly impressed by the new abstract painting there, its impact was not really felt until the advent of several important exhibitions in London, the first of which, organised by the Museum of Modern Art, was held at the Tate Gallery in 1956. Specific parallels can be drawn between the subsequent work of a number of British artists and their American counterparts, but there can be no doubt that, in general terms, the influence of New York was reflected almost immediately in the larger canvases, freer and more expressive handling of paint and bolder colours

William Scott, **Ochre Painting** 1958

Alan Davie, **Sacrifice** 1956

which came to characterise British art of the later 1950s and the sixties. These tendencies were, however, modified by the generally softer and more lyrical approach of the British. An exception is perhaps Alan Davie, whose works were initially influenced by Pollock's expressionist and barbaric paintings of 1942–5, which he had seen in Venice as early as 1948. Pollock's clashes of movement and fragmentary images suggestive of primitive rituals are echoed in such works as 'Sacrifice', 1956, a sombre image suggesting orgiastic pagan rites. The absorption of American Abstract Expressionist influences and their transformation into something more European is illustrated by the work of Patrick Heron, whose 'Brown Ground with Soft Red and Green: August 1958–July 1959' shows the influence of Rothko, but differs from American painting in its asymmetry, its greater complexity and in the use of advancing and receding colour areas. His work has since tended to become more and more different from that of the Americans.

Roger Hilton, **Oi Yoi Yoi** 1963

Pop Art

The term Pop Art originally referred to the commercial or popular arts by contrast with fine art, and it was an interest in this area which led some artists in Britain to borrow some of the motifs and techniques to make their own fine art. This new form of fine art came to be called 'Pop Art', and the term has since been used to cover the works of a number of mostly British and American artists, who were never linked as a group but shared this common theme. Indeed, this was a theme that became prominent throughout Western culture in the late 1950s with the rise of popular music and the growth of interest in pulp magazines, commercial films and the worlds of fashion, advertising and communications. Pop Art, like Post-Painterly Abstraction, marked a move away from Abstract Expressionism, away from the more anxious and soul-baring paintings of the 1940s towards the 'cooler' sensibility of the 1960s. However, like Abstract Expressionism, it incorporated an emphasis on 'process' and like all modern art it was partly concerned to question the nature of art as well as the world around.

Pop Art in Britain started quite independently from the new work in America. The British origins are in the Independent Group, a group of artists, designers, art critics, architects and even a band leader, which first met at the Institute of Contemporary Arts in 1952. Their second lecture given by Eduardo Paolozzi was entitled 'Bunk', a weird and massive presentation through an epidiascope of 'found' images from both technological sources and popular magazines. These images were related to the collages he had been making since 1947 when as a student in Paris he had seen the work of Ernst and Duchamp and mixed this influence with his admiration for sex and cinema magazine images, American comics, food and automobile advertisements. In 1956 members of the Independent group helped create an exhibition at the Whitechapel Art Gallery called 'This is Tomorrow', and it was the poster for this exhibition designed by Richard Hamilton which has often been regarded as the first work of Pop Art.

Hamilton had been concerned with several didactic exhibitions including 'Growth and Form' in 1951 and 'Man, Machine and Motion' in 1955. In 1957 Hamilton defined in a letter what he thought Pop Art meant to him: 'popular (designed for mass audience); transient (short term solution); expendable (easily forgotten); low cost; mass produced; young (aimed at youth); witty; sexy; gimmicky; glamorous; and last but not least, big business'. His own art began to combine his extensive knowledge of popular culture with his skills as a painter and his particular intellectual flair, while beginning to correspond with some of the adjectives above. Hamilton made '$he' after making two works which explored American automobile styling and female sexuality. In an exposition of the work written in 1962 he explained that he saw the relation between woman and domestic appliances as an obsessive and archetypal theme of our culture. The work is concerned with the manipulation of our ways of seeing by the different types of admass techniques, especially photography. Here we see elements drawn from a pin-up photograph and advertisements for kitchen equipment, but in a composition and with paint technique as deliber-

Richard Hamilton, $he 1958–61

ate as a Cézanne or Giacometti. Fantasy plays an important part in this and other Pop works and Lawrence Alloway wrote, in 1958, that 'Fantasy resides in, to sample a few examples, film stars, perfume ads, beauty and the beast situations, terrible deaths and sexy women . . . However, Fantasy is always given a keen topical edge; the sexy model is shaped by datable fashion as well as by timeless lust. Thus, the mass arts orient the

Peter Blake, **On the Balcony** 1955–7

R.B. Kitaj, **Isaac Babel riding with Budyonny** 1962

consumer in current styles, even when they seem purely, timelessly erotic and fantastic. The mass media give perpetual lessons in assimilation, instruction in role-taking, the use of new objects, the definition of changing relationships . . .'

Although he was one of the pioneers of Pop Art in Britain, Peter Blake is essentially a traditional painter who has been fascinated by the entertainment industry, popular heroes, pin-ups and folk culture. He painted 'On the Balcony' while he was still a student at the Royal College of Art, which was the art school where the majority of Pop artists studied and met each other. Children are depicted holding different pictures in different styles, while they sit on a balcony (there are a number of other forms of this theme in the picture). The accumulation of badges, the carefully painted photographic images and incorporation of magazine covers and cult heroes, which here include the Royal Family, all contribute to its Pop imagery. Blake's works often include a nostalgia for a child-like dream, a wonderment at the world and are some of the most straightforward pieces of adulation of popular culture, a position very close to some of the American West Coast artists such as Ed Ruscha. Richard Smith and Joe Tilson were students at the Royal College at the same time as Blake. Smith's interest in the motifs, style and packaging of consumer products has always linked him with the Pop painters, but the degree of abstraction, the formal and painterly beauty of his works have equally placed them in the field of Post-Painterly Abstraction. After travelling to New York in 1959, he developed his most 'Pop' works with a soft-focus style that recreated the thin dazzle of the glamorous advertisement. Tilson has often incorporated stencil-like, cut out letters into his paintings, such as 'Vox Box', where image and title are read simultaneously.

The next generation of Pop artists were at the Royal College between 1959 and 1962, and made a considerable impact at the Young Contemporaries exhibition in 1961. These included R.B. Kitaj, Peter Phillips, Allen Jones, David Hockney, Derek Boshier and Patrick Caulfield. By the time they left college 'Pop' images were becoming fashionable and were beginning to be incorporated into 'Swinging London'. Both Jones and Hockney have spoken of the influence of Kitaj, an American with a wide and varied education who had come to live in London. Kitaj's paintings use references from beyond the Pop world, and contain a sometimes disturbing mixture of the historical, intellectual and surreal. Hockney has said that it was Kitaj who encouraged him to use his own life and the objects around him for the subject matter of his paintings, and that he then had no longer to worry about the abstract-figurative dilemma. He became fascinated with painting in different styles and came to understand that it was unnecessary to paint on the whole canvas and that he could use different parts for different kinds of

Roy Lichtenstein
Whaam! 1963
Acrylic on canvas,
68 × 160 (172.7 × 406.4)

Roy Lichtenstein started to paint 'Pop' imagery from 1961, and the use of comic strip images was one of the most important categories in his work up until 1965. He said in 1967 that, 'At that time I was interested in anything I could use as a subject that was emotionally strong – usually love, war or something that was highly-charged or emotional subject matter. Also I wanted the subject matter to be opposite to the removed and deliberate paint-techniques. Cartooning itself usually consists of very highly-charged subject matter carried out in standard, obvious and removed techniques.' The process of transfer of the image from the comic book to the painting involves further simplification and stylisation of an image, and this together with the division into two canvases and the enormous alteration in scale separate the painting from an actual comic strip: they are not paintings of a strip, but firmly based on the allusion. As Lichtenstein says: 'I want my images to be as critical, as threatening, and as insistent as possible'.

'Whaam!' has a particularly strong contrast between the vehemence and brutality of the image and the cool detachment of the pictorial and typographic style, and between the illusion of depth in space and the flatness of the picture plane. These contrasts are even more specific to explosions: 'It is true that they may have some kind of form at any particular moment, but they are never totally perceived as defined shape. Cartoonists have developed explosions into specific forms. That's why I also like to do them in three dimensions.' The explosion fills the whole of the right-hand canvas and the artist wrote, 'I remember being concerned with the idea of doing two almost separate paintings having little hint of compositional connection, and each having slightly separate stylistic character. Of course there is the humorous connection of one panel shooting the other . . .
The heroes depicted in comic books are fascist types, but I don't take them seriously in these paintings – maybe there is a point in not taking them seriously, a political point. I use them for purely formal reasons, and that's not what those heroes were invented for.'

marks, including drawing and graffiti. Hockney's painting style has since become more unified, but an important part of his work has continued to be drawing and etching. Allen Jones' paintings swing between illusion and abstraction, using shaped canvases and a painterly style which is half about painting itself. He has used eroticism and sexuality as a common and almost neutral theme with which to expose visual conventions, and to make an imaginary world into which to draw the spectator. Peter Phillips has continued to make Pop paintings in the 1970s, and in the early 1960s his works were, like those of Anthony Donaldson, very akin to American paintings in their self-conscious collage of cult motifs, combined in a highly coloured and decorative style. While Patrick Caulfield never considered himself a Pop artist (he was associated because his paintings appeared to lean heavily on techniques from graphic design), Derek Boshier only had a short period making specifically Pop paintings, often featuring man as some kind of automaton.

Jasper Johns, **Zero through Nine** 1961

The origins of Pop Art in America were much less coherent than in Britain. There was a strong initial influence from Jasper Johns and Robert Rauschenberg, who from 1955 were working in close association but in distinctive styles. Johns started to make use of striking but commonplace images such as flags, maps, targets or numbers which are flat and graphic in character and therefore bring a profound ambiguity into the relationship of image and object. 'Zero through Nine', for instance, includes the numbers from 0 to 9 superimposed, but is painted with a sensuous, intricate web of brushstrokes and contrasting colours. Rauschenberg developed the use of silk-screen printing on to canvas, allowing the repetitive use of photographic images which he linked together by passages of free brushwork. He also made many extraordinary 'combines' which broke down the barriers between painting and sculpture through the application of paint to real objects. They were both interested in the work of Marcel Duchamp, who had lived in America since the First World War, and his influence, with that of Dada and Surrealism, provided a common background for the American Pop artists. The paintings of Stuart Davis and Gerald Murphy, which had featured brand name products in the 1920s, and those of Larry Rivers in the 1950s which incorporated themes and images close to Pop, although his style remained painterly and 'high-art', were similarly influential. In the generation after Abstract Expressionism, 'Junk-Art' or Assemblage provided the possibility of an art that was also American, but concerned not with the personal conflicts of the artist, nor with beautiful or heroic things, but with the city and its objects.

It was this theme which concerned Claes Oldenburg and Jim Dine in the 'Happenings', semi-spontaneous, semi-scripted live performances, which they presented in New York in 1959 and 1960. Allan Kaprow, who had invented the term 'Happenings', had originally called his events 'Action-Collages' and in their loose juxtaposition of diverse objects and performers they were close to the spirit of Assemblage. In 1961 Oldenburg rented a real shop and made 'The Store' where he presented over a hundred rather ambiguous chunky objects, mostly items of clothing and food like 'Counter and Plates with Potato and Ham', made of plaster on a wire frame and painted in cheap, bright, enamel paints. These objects, and those presented in an earlier environment called 'The Street', showed some influence from Dubuffet in their cheap and debased materials and their connection with the unregarded things of the city. He made more installations and Happenings and only gradually began to regard some of his objects as having an independent and individual existence as sculptures. He became more and more concerned with scale, and with making objects which mimic commercial manufacture and are often a humorous parody of their 'real' appearance. The 'Soft Drainpipe – Blue (Cool) Version' could be a phallic symbol, a crucifix or a T-shape. This T-shape is a doubled version of the 'Ray Gun' shape that has endlessly fascinated Oldenburg. His changes of scale and isolation of types of object have led him to consider public

Claes Oldenburg,
Soft Drainpipe–Blue (Cool) Version 1967

brilliant colours – the face mauve, the hair yellow, the eyelids green and the background orange – and those on the right screenprinted in black and white. As in all his paintings of her, the head is based on a photograph of her taken in 1953, as publicity for the film *Niagara*.

James Rosenquist studied art at college, also worked as an industrial painter, painting vast areas of garages and warehouses, and learned the art of sign-painting through painting bill boards for an advertising company. From 1960 he found a style where he could get away from the traditional relationships of scale and space. The qualities of that style are the great scale, the juxtaposition of fragmentary images mostly taken from picture magazines and their execution in a smooth, high-keyed manner like the photographs and drawn illustrations of the magazines. Jim Dine, who was involved with Happenings in the late sixties, continued in his drawing and painting to use fine art techniques but applied them to individual, ordinary objects, like clothes or tools.

monuments, such as his proposal for a set of giant lipsticks for Piccadilly Circus.

While making drawings of cartoon characters and a picture of Donald Duck for his two sons, Roy Lichtenstein realised that this could make a serious work, and with the encouragement of Allan Kaprow he started to make his first pictures from comic-strips. Although aware of the nature and meaning of his sources, Lichtenstein has always been concerned with the process of converting them into pictures, with their formal and pictorial qualities and with the implications of presenting them as art. Whereas Lichtenstein's works are beautifully hand-painted, Andy Warhol has since 1961 used entirely 'commercial' techniques in the production of his art. His art, and from 1965, his films, have always been simultaneously banal and sensational (using themes such as death, heroes and sex), produced with considerable distortion in colour but in a flat non-illusionistic manner which highlights the cult-personality of someone like Marilyn Monroe, rather than involving any attempt at a traditional representation. His 'Marilyn Diptych' made in 1962, the year of her death, comprises two large canvases with series of heads of Marilyn Monroe arranged in rows, those on the left-hand panel painted in

British Painting and Sculpture after 1960

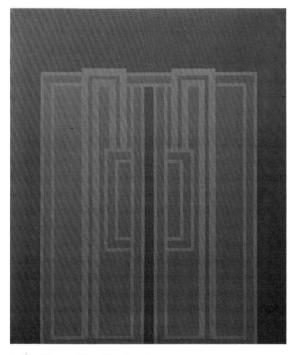

Robyn Denny, **Life Line I** 1963

Despite the notable increase in artistic activity in Great Britain in the late 1950s, which brought with it an increase in contemporary art galleries and exhibitions, in 1960 a group of younger artists felt that their large abstract paintings were not being seen by the public, and so financed and arranged the exhibition called 'Situation' at the R.B.A. Galleries in London. It succeeded in marking out a generation both younger and with different aims from the abstract and semi-abstract painters of St Ives. The committee was chaired by Lawrence Alloway and included Bernard Cohen, William Turnbull and Robyn Denny. The common ground among the artists was the nature of their abstraction (no visual representation at all) and the size of their canvases (not less than thirty square feet). In his introduction to the catalogue Roger Coleman stressed three fundamental values. First, that the artists wished to create, in relation to the spectator, a new conception of space by 'surrounding'

him or her with a painting that was on the same scale as the environment. Secondly, that the paintings could be regarded as a record of a sequence of actions, though none of them were 'action' paintings, and had not usually involved previous planning. Thirdly, that through their strong commitment to the act of painting, and in the motifs they were using, the artists were striving to give painting an existence in its own right, not based on a representation of another reality. It was clear that the new developments in American painting (first shown at the Tate Gallery in 1956 and more extensively in 1959) and the development of British abstract painting, and in particular the work of Patrick Heron and Terry Frost, had been absorbed and understood by the younger painters. They wished to turn away from the conventions of abstract landscape painting, away from the prevailing English mood, and we see in their works a new 'coolness' and an appetite for American culture which was equally apparent in the newly emerging Pop Art of the time. Their canvases are characterised by the use of less gestural brushstrokes, the predominance of relatively schematic and clear compositions, and a heightened awareness of the relation between colour and illusion.

Both Robyn Denny and Richard Smith contributed in 1959 to an exhibition called 'Place' where their abstract paintings were exhibited as a free-standing zig-zag shaped environment through which the public walked. From 1960 Denny's paintings are between six and eight feet high, hung near the ground, with an emphasis on symmetry and emblematic structure, a very distinct change from his works of the mid to late fifties which had involved collage and stencilled words, based on his interest in theories of communication. The new work, often sombre in tone, involved, in contrast to Richard Smith, the precise, hard-edged marking of rectilinear forms, floating in a background, coming forward and back with the colours either merging or producing exact contrasts. This structural concern for the ambiguity between figure and ground, surface and illusion, is always

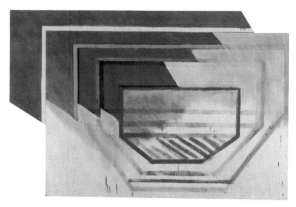

Richard Smith, **Vista** 1963

Bernard Cohen, **Matter of Identity I** 1963

balanced by the creation of a strong overall mood. Smith was directly connected with the second generation of British Pop artists emerging from the Royal College of Art in the late 1950s and his work reflected a strong interest in packaged products and advertisements. In 1959 he went to New York on a Harkness Fellowship and there he painted works in a style like soft-focus photography, that mimicked the cool but glossy atmosphere of the American consumer-orientated image. 'Vista' marks a more concentrated concern with illusion and recession, together with an interest in box-like shapes and packages, and is one of the first 'shaped' canvases made in Britain. Smith further explored this theme by making a series of works which use an actual three-dimensional box-shaped canvas as part of a painting. These often utilise the shape of a cigarette packet (in 'Gift Wrap' and 'Piano') and are on a strange borderline between painting and sculpture. In recent years he has made paintings without a wooden stretcher, substituting a light frame similar to a kite, and has sewn and hung the paintings in a variety of different ways thus exposing the work's whole structure. Both Smith's and Denny's paintings reflected the new sensibility of the 1960s where the artist no longer needed to 'bare the soul', but could take a detached look at the world around (while remaining closely involved) and present new images which connect with the apparently more affluent and less anxious society that existed in Britain for a few years.

This same cool detachment can be seen in the work of Paul Huxley, Jeremy Moon and Mark Lancaster, all of whom have used bright colours and clear, bold designs, and a deliberation that suppressed the Expressionist connotations of colour. Their work has involved different shapes and sizes of canvas, and a common search for abstract designs that are visually seductive. Bernard Cohen, perhaps more eclectic and more personal in his approach, was teaching at Ealing School of Art between 1961 and 1964. A concern for making different types of visual language, for understanding the visual codes in drawing and design, and a strong interest in cybernetics (the speciality of Roy Ascott who ran the course at Ealing) all permeated Cohen's work at this period. 'Matter of Identity I' is divided into different stylistic parts, many of which overlap, which allows the spectator to read different parts separately and to formulate several 'compositions'. In any painting Cohen exposes the processes by which it was made, the passage of time and a rich subconscious fantasy. By comparison, Ian Stephenson has worked to create unified images, in which the distribution and density of the drops of paint are precisely controlled to contrast a conspicuous surface with spatial illusion and atmospheric mood.

While keeping a strong measure of deliberation, both John Hoyland and John Walker have introduced a considerable degree of spontaneity in their work. Having provided himself with a structure Hoyland works on to

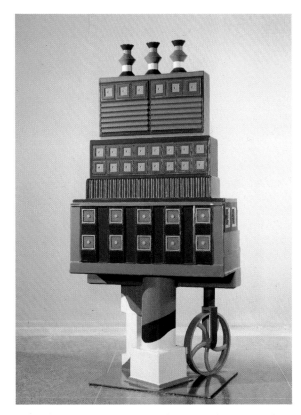

Eduardo Paolozzi,
The City of the Circle and the Square 1963/1966

explore density and extent of colour, a concern that was most important in Hans Hofmann's paintings, and to exploit the almost sculptural potential of drips and sections of acrylic paint. John Walker worked for some years in a kind of semi-figurative abstraction, using a mysterious motif like a piece of folded paper, painted on top of a grid-like pattern. In the mid 1960s he changed to the use of trapezoid, rhomboid and triangular shapes both within and as the actual format for his paintings.

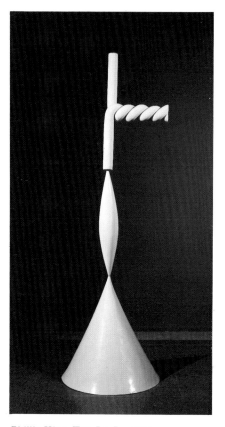

Phillip King, **Tra-La-La** 1963

Anthony Caro's abstract sculpture, inaugurated in 1960 with 'Twenty-Four Hours', was influential through his teaching and through the climate of sculptural experiment that he encouraged, as well as through his actual works. Works of William Turnbull and Eduardo Paolozzi had already displayed many of the stylistic characteristics that came into prominence in the 1960s. Turnbull made in the mid to late 1950s totemic structures, still anthropomorphic, which stood directly on the ground and which often combined carving with bronze castings, the most extreme of which were highly simplified, Brancusi-inspired 'heads' and 'idols'. During the 1960s his work became even more stringent and structural, quiet but insistent in its clear, bright colours and logical

progressions. Paolozzi had in the 1950s made assemblage sculptures from junk metal and machine parts, and in the early 1960s developed a series of works which were manufactured under his direction in a specialised engineering workshop. 'The City of the Circle and the Square' is an example of these sculptures which were constructed from casts in aluminium and gunmetal and painted in bright 'Pop' colours. Both George Fullard and Bruce Lacey were making sculptures from junk at this time, Lacey's works being sharply satirical comments on current issues.

The younger generation of abstract sculptors from St Martin's School of Art were given a prominent position in the New Generation sculpture exhibition at the Whitechapel Art Gallery in 1965. The general use of new materials, plastics, fibreglass and aluminium, was evident, not as an exposition of any theory of 'truth to materials', but rather to create various visual and sculptural effects and as part of the breaking down of the separate categories of painting and sculpture (the kinship with painting being emphasised by the widespread use of vivid colour). The new materials often allowed an immediacy of creation that was never possible with bronze or stone, and showed connections with painting through the influence of Matisse's paper cutouts. William Tucker defined the concerns of the younger sculptors when he wrote in 1969: 'It was not until the last few years that a sculpture started to emerge that disowned the monumental, the precious, the animate – all those qualities that tend to remove sculpture from the object-world. It rested directly on the ground – was not elevated on a pedestal – and was made from inexpensive, easily available material, the quality of which was unimportant except in so far as it bodied the formal quality of the object, and which in any case was usually concealed by an opaque skin of paint. The sculpture object was finally freed from the residual structure of the human figure, the inhibitions of expensive materials and complex craft processes.' These qualities are all present in Tucker's own work and that of Phillip King, Tim Scott, David Annesley and Michael Bolus. King's 'Tra-la-la', which is made of painted fibreglass, utilises the shape of the cone which has been one of his recurrent preoccupations. Its forthright thinness and vertical extent make it visually surprising, stretching the limits of our ordinary appreciation of sculpture.

Much as the exceptional power of statement of Moore and Hepworth had produced a healthy reaction in the works of their assistants (Anthony Caro, Phillip King), so the challenging work of this generation produced a major reaction in its turn. A reaction where the substance and meaning of sculpture were challenged.

Barry Flanagan was another student of St Martin's School of Art (a contemporary of Richard Long, Bruce McLean, Gilbert and George and Hamish Fulton) who

Anthony Caro
Early One Morning 1962
Painted steel, 114 × 244 × 132
(289.6 × 619.8 × 335.3)

In 1960 Anthony Caro made a radical break with the modelled and bronze cast sculptures of the human form that he had made in the preceding years. He started to construct metal sculptures which were completely abstract, but had a richness and complexity that could induce in the spectator sensations similar to those experienced when viewing a work which recreates the human body. 'Early One Morning' is one of the largest of the works made in the early sixties, but is made, like all these sculptures, to be viewed in an interior space so that one is forced physically into a close relationship with the work. In such a way, one views it as a three-dimensional composition which appears to alter as one walks around it. Its composition and size (over twenty feet long by eleven wide), though still essentially on a human scale, are sufficient to make views from different angles surprisingly dissimilar. The whole is more than a sum of the parts.

It is made of steel and aluminium, bolted and welded together and painted with a uniform coat of gloss paint. It was constructed by the addition of parts, either standard industrial sections or parts of scrap metal, without any maquette or preparatory drawings. Caro has explained this procedure by saying: 'I have a piece in my studio, and it strikes me as being O.K.; but that it just needs something – or maybe a number of things to make it work. Very much like a note, to which you add another note and you finally have a piece of music . . .' The 'openness' and harmony of this composition act to give an appearance of weightlessness in the sculpture, as if it is suspended in the air, an effect which is in direct contrast to the monumentality of most traditional, pedestal-supported sculptures. The sharp colour contributes to this sensation, acting to unify the different shapes of the parts and to neutralise the material or surface character of individual and diverse elements. The colour also serves to set the mood for the work, giving a bright and optimistic prospect which is corroborated by the title.

was interested in exploring the use of less rigid and permanent materials and testing the limits of three dimensions. From 1965 he made works from hessian, canvas and plaster, like 'aaing i gui aa' which in their squatness, subdued and soaked colour and use of the surreal or fantastic were quite different from the works of the generation above. In 1967 he started to use sand and made tall columns in which the sand supported the canvas and the canvas supported the sand, combined with manufactured materials like rope and linoleum. The concern for the integrity of materials, for not disguising

Barry Flanagan, **aaing i gui aa** 1965

them with paint or intricate shape, has characterised the work of some younger sculptors such as Nicholas Pope.

The period of the middle to late 1960s gave a public prominence to abstract styles, but the use of figurative traditions has always remained very strong in Britain. In part it was given impetus by Pop Art, whose painters, Richard Hamilton, Peter Blake, David Hockney, Allen Jones and Peter Phillips, although not producing work in any definable pop manner after 1963 (with the exception of Peter Phillips) continued in the use of strong figurative imagery. In part it was the acceptance and success of a number of diverse painters who had been associated however loosely with Pop such as R.B. Kitaj, Michael Andrews, Howard Hodgkin and Patrick Caulfield. In part it was the continuation of a figurative style which had grown up at the Euston Road School and

was still taught at the Slade School of Art, its exponents including Euan Uglow and Patrick George, and in part the legacy of Bomberg in the strong paintings of Frank Auerbach and Leon Kossoff. Kitaj's work has always been intellectually stimulating with frequent references to politics, philosophy and history combined in an intense style which he has strongly defended as the best means of conveying his meanings, both private and public. Both Michael Andrews and Patrick Caulfield use figurative imagery with very severe formal controls, but whereas Andrews' paintings have a dream-like ambiguity, Caulfield's appear to represent a stylised reality of the artist's own creation. His precision in line and form, and his clear non-illusionistic colouring have always emphasised the symbolic and timeless nature of all his subject matter together with his fascination with *styles* in the culture as a whole. In 'After Lunch' the insistent sense of the surreal is heightened by the picture within a picture, painted in the style of the Super-Realists. Howard Hodgkin's paintings use very private subject matter, a moment of special concentration for the artist, like a particular meal with friends, or the ambience in a room. He does not represent it but makes intense encapsulations with a strange vivid use of paint all the way from the 'crude' to the lyrically delicate. The young abstract painter Stephen Buckley has much in common in technique with Hodgkin and similarly juxtaposes bright areas of colour (in the tradition of Matisse), but extends this to making constructions in which canvases and stretchers play an equal part with paint. This kind of

Patrick Caulfield, **After Lunch** 1975

David Hockney
Mr and Mrs Clark and Percy 1970–1
Acrylic on canvas,
84 × 120 (213.4 × 304.8)

This is one of a series of double portraits which Hockney has painted of his friends, all of which are seven feet by ten feet. It portrays Ossie Clark, the fashion designer, and his wife, Celia Birtwell, the fabric designer. They are shown with Percy, one of their two white cats, in front of an open window in the drawing room of their London home. The series has included portraits of Christopher Isherwood with Don Bachardy (1968), and Henry Geldzahler with Christopher Scott (1968/9). They were all painted by Hockney's choice rather than as commissions.

The final work was painted from small drawings, from many black and white and coloured photographs of the Clarks and the room (many of which have been donated by the artist to the Tate) and also directly from life. The photographic studies include Celia Birtwell's head, the position of her hand on her hip, Ossie Clark in the chair on each side of the window, the window itself, chairs, tables, lamps and telephone. The lilies were painted from life in the artist's studio, where he had set them up in light conditions similar to those of the drawing room. An interesting feature is the depiction on the wall of one of Hockney's own etchings, one of the plates from 'A Rake's Progress'. Hockney did not decide on the pose of the couple but painted them in a position in which he knew they often placed themselves. He has said that Celia Birtwell's dress, hair, gaze and position suggested to him a portrait in the classical style, but the convention has been reversed here, in that it is the woman who stands while the man sits.

Hockney deliberately simplified the appearance of the room where the couple chose to be painted: there had been more objects on the table and a picture hung on the right-hand wall. He wished to convey with particular clarity both the illusion of space and the fall of light and the ambience of this interior. Hockney has often used his own life as the source material for his paintings, and it is important to him to make paintings about friends and places he knows. Parallel with this personal involvement is a fascination with recording the objects, style and setting of a contemporary scene. The self-conscious expressions on the faces of the couple as well as their own choice of semi-formal pose, seem to give an indication of their own interests and work: designing fashionable clothes where image and appearance are all important.

investigation of structure and materials may also be seen in Keith Milow's work.

Tom Phillips and Rita Donagh both use a combination of visual mechanisms, both abstract and figurative, to convey themes and ideas in their work. Tom Phillip's 'Benches' was taken from picture postcards of benches in municipal parks in various British cities. The transitory nature of life was suggested to him by the anonymous figures transfixed for a moment in the equally anonymous postcard, present on one occasion on a sunny day but not present when the bench was next photographed. Phillips has often used quite extensive texts in his works, and here a shortened text from St Peter's gospel: 'For all flesh is as grass, the grass withereth' is painted next to the postcard manufacturer's code numbers. The stripes are a catalogue of colours used in painting, their widths determined entirely by chance. Rita Donagh combines an almost completely abstract system with highly particular and selected newspaper photographs, often tragic images from Northern Ireland. The system is sometimes abstracted from other systems like maps (of such things as sites of Celtic burial chambers) and is painted against a schematised room perspective. Donagh's work like that of Kitaj and Phillips is typical of a continuing concern for human and political issues, expressed not simply by reflecting the motifs and signs of current culture, but through the transformation of images by which the spectator is led to question their meaning (a concern that was pioneered by Richard Hamilton's work in the 1950s), and part of a more general tendency in the art of the 1970s towards the reintroduction of the personal world and opinions of the artist.

Tom Phillips, **Benches** 1970–1

Minimal, Conceptual and other new art

Mark Boyle, **Holland Park Avenue Study** 1967

In 1959 Carl Andre was sharing a part of Frank Stella's studio and started to make simple vertical carvings, of which 'Last Ladder' is one, principally composed of a number of repetitive cuts into a beam of wood. He was influenced by the carvings of Brancusi, but wished to make 'negative sculpture' by emphasising the cuts in something rather than the shaping of a new form. Early in the next year Anthony Caro started to make radically abstract sculptures which, unlike Andre's carvings, were assembled from pieces of discarded industrial metal, but similarly stood directly on the ground. Some influence from David Smith and Kenneth Noland is apparent in Caro's first abstract sculpture, 'Twenty-Four Hours', and it was this work which led him on to a method of working which was very influential during the 1960s. But whereas Caro was at this time making sculptures in which the parts were set off against each other as a composition, Andre was making works which were symmetrical, where each part was equal and a simple method of working was made clear. This was a similar approach to that of Stella and Noland who used symmetrical, all-over designs in their paintings.

During the 1960s sculpture became more generally accepted as an important part of the development of modern art. This was, in part, because sculptors had blatantly broken with the conventions of the public monument to which their work had traditionally been attached (although modern sculptures began to be more frequently commissioned with new modern buildings) and refused to be limited to the scale of the domestic. Artists and critics became aware that however abstract the design of a painting, it was impossible to exclude all illusion when presenting colour and shape on a two-dimensional plane. Sculpture was free of this problem because it was an object and could *be* abstract form with no implication of spatial illusion. This recognition of the 'reality of objects' was connected with a desire to make clear in the completed work of art the method by which it was made. This emphasis on process, originally pioneered by Pollock's paintings of the 1940s, was also made apparent in Actions, Performances and Happenings where artists claimed that their art *was* the act of making (or destroying) something. The works of Robert Morris often aim to reveal no more than their structure, though

his four mirror cubes, first made in 1965, incorporate a contradiction between their very clear-cut geometrical forms and the mirrored surfaces which reflect the viewers and gallery around them. His works with felt and other soft materials, emphasise both the process by which they were brought together, and the shape and orientation of the surfaces which support them. Using more dense and rigid material Richard Serra has leaned a sheet and roll of lead against the wall as in 'Shovel Plate Prop', or splashed molten lead into the junction between a wall and a floor forming a sculpture almost simultaneous with impact. The common concern about the surrounding space of a sculpture allied with a strong sense of the mysterious, is emphasised in reverse by Bruce Nauman's 'Corridor with Mirror and White Lights' which comprises a strongly illuminated and impenetrable narrow space, and the work of Walter de Maria in which he covered a gallery floor with earth (Galerie Heiner Friedrich, Munich, September 1968). This concern has often been present in the work of Barry Flanagan, and more recently in that of Nigel Hall and Tim Head. Other aspects of this interest in environment are to be seen in the works of Christo, which have involved wrapping buildings and making a twenty-five mile cloth fence, and those of Mark Boyle which are perfect reproductions of randomly selected sections of the surface of the earth.

The exposition of structure, an idea in part borrowed from the tradition of Constructivism and in part from Abstract Expressionism, has been used by artists in many media, including film, performance, video, dance and music. It is a central part of the aesthetic of Minimal Art, a term coined in about 1965 for the more reductive tendencies in sculpture and painting. The theory of minimalism is that without the diverting presence of 'composition', and by the use of plain, often industrial, materials arranged in geometrical or highly simplified configurations we may experience all the more strongly the pure qualities of colour, form, space and materials. Thus less may, so to speak, equal more. Donald Judd has used wood, coloured plexiglass or bright copper, all relatively sensuous materials but has combined them in such clear and rigorous ways that material and order are emphasised as qualities in themselves without any external reference. He has frequently made reliefs deliberately to avoid any direct confusion with either painting or sculpture. His works are designed in advance and fabricated by industrial specialists. The use of skilled technicians as the fabricators of art works, in which Judd, Sol LeWitt and Eduardo Paolozzi have taken a particular interest, emphasises a structural concern with the precise definitions of a specification which in turn stresses art as the idea which need be given actual form only when required. Sol LeWitt had 'Two Open Modular Cubes/Half-Off' made from standard aluminium units which were given a plain baked enamel finish to concentrate the viewer's attention on the scale, geometry and formation of the work, the art lying in the arrangement and structure of the grid rather than any handwork. His Wall Drawings, which can be accommodated on

Sol LeWitt, **Two Open Modular Cubes/Half-Off** 1970

different sized walls and can attain a strange and overpowering effect, only exist as art works when they have been drawn out on the wall, a process usually carried out by trained assistants in accordance with his specifications.

Carl Andre integrated his sculpture with a gallery space when he filled a gallery (Dwan Gallery, Los Angeles, 1967) with a layer of concrete blocks and then removed rectangles, leaving shapes in negative: sculpture as a 'cut in space'. These shapes were like negative versions of a group of eight brick sculptures he had already made, of which 'Equivalent VIII' is one. They

Carl Andre, **Equivalent VIII** 1966

were all composed of 120 fire bricks arranged in two layers in different combinations (3 × 20, 4 × 15, 5 × 12 and so on), which made rectangular shapes which were visually surprisingly varied but, of course, occupied exactly the same volume. Here Andre uses the brick as an object whose form is prescribed, to build shapes where a perceptual whole is made up of units simply laid together, and where the lowness of the shape contrasts with the upright and vertical orientation of most traditional sculpture. With this work and '144 Magnesium Plates' the direct use of previously made, standard materials does not preclude an appreciation of the ordinary aesthetic qualities of works of art: beauty of colour, form and texture. Dan Flavin combines fluorescent tubes in works which are both material and immaterial. The 'Monument for V. Tatlin' is a romantic homage to the Constructivist pioneer, and uses an almost Art Deco style in a wall-hung configuration. Larry Bell has worked extensively with glass which is partly mirrored and partly transparent, both in the construction of small boxes and environmental works which contradict one's first viewing by the use of both internal and external reflection. William Turnbull and Carel Visser have both made sculptures which use rectangular and cuboid shapes as the basic unit with which to build structures.

Reductive or Minimal painting of the 1960s and 1970s has various important predecessors, including the white Suprematist paintings of Malevich, the 'achromes' of Piero Manzoni and Yves Klein's blue paintings. The later paintings of Ad Reinhardt involved a deliberate attempt to make an 'ultimate painting', an aim which had evolved from his view of the development of Western art. In practice he mixed red, blue and green paint with matt black to produce resonantly black paintings which have often been regarded as some of the most extreme minimal paintings. The paintings of Agnes Martin and Bob Law, the former composed of soft lines in a grid pattern and the latter of layer after layer of dark blue or violet paint,

Frank Stella
Six Mile Bottom 1960
Metallic paint on canvas,
$118\frac{1}{8} \times 71\frac{3}{4}$ (300 × 182.2)

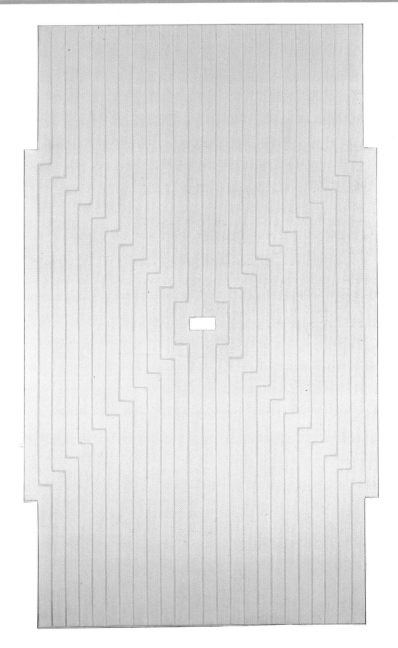

The American painter Frank Stella, who was born in 1936, began his career at a time when Abstract Expressionism was the dominant style and his work tends, like Abstract Expressionist pictures, to be large in scale. However the two series of black and aluminium pictures painted in 1959–60 with which he first made his reputation marked a radical departure from Abstract Expressionism and were an important influence on the subsequent Minimalist movement of the 1960s. Instead of working in an improvisatory way and making radical changes as he went along, these pictures were all planned in advance and were painted in accordance with a predetermined system. Instead of having free brushwork, they were executed in uniform parallel stripes applied as flatly as possible.

The black series, which was executed in 1959–60, consisted of paintings entirely covered with a simple regular symmetrical design of black stripes of uniform width; the stripes were all either in a vertical-horizontal orientation (echoing the rectangular format) or parallel to the diagonals (cutting across it). In the aluminium series which followed immediately afterwards, Stella carried yet further the relationship between the composition and the picture format. Instead of using straight bands, he designed pictures with bands which jogged to one side and then turned again to resume their original direction. By applying this principle consistently throughout he arrived at compositions which had small rectangular spaces 'left over' at the edges or in the centre, or both. After some initial hesitation, he decided to omit these 'left-over' sections altogether and to make stretchers of irregular shapes. 'Six Mile Bottom' is one of the only two works out of the series of eight to have a hole in the centre and therefore marks a particularly significant stage in the development of the shaped canvas.

The fact that these aluminium pictures were painted in accordance with a set of rules that the artist had set himself beforehand, and that these rules could be deduced by anyone who looked at the pictures with sufficient care, represented a development of considerable significance. Moreover their cool, impersonal character was enhanced by the use of metallic paint normally reserved for painting radiators and by the deep, heavy stretchers which gave the pictures something of the appearance of slab-like objects.

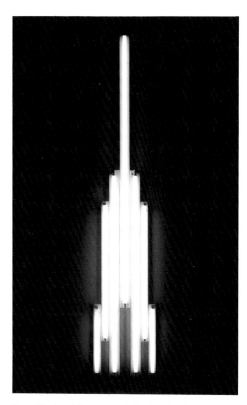

Dan Flavin, **'Monument' for V. Tatlin** 1966–9

have references in the artist's intention, like works of Barnett Newman, which go beyond the formalist concerns outlined above. Martin's paintings are analogues for states of mind or sensations. She has written that with 'Morning' she was painting about happiness and bliss. Law's work also concerns a philosophic search for perfection which is expressed in making successive 'black' paintings in each of which the capabilities of the medium are stretched to their limit.

Conceptual art may be seen as part of a more general tendency towards what has been referred to as the dematerialisation of art. Many artists in the mid 1960s sought once again to question the nature of the whole of art, to investigate its boundaries and to incorporate many systems and ideas in life which had never previously been associated with art. While essentially being concerned with human life and society, all this art underlined the central importance of theory, and began to use photographs and texts, which had previously appeared in or been adjuncts to works of art, as common tools of art practice. The sources of conceptual art in its many forms are extremely diverse. Although the influence of Marcel Duchamp was more specific in the work of Jasper Johns and already effective in the creation of Pop Art, it continued to be of widespread importance throughout the 1960s. His attitude stressed the importance of the artist

himself and the use of (sometimes esoteric) theory; as he said: 'I wanted to put painting once again at the service of the mind.' His Ready-mades, first produced in 1913, which involved the nomination and appropriation of objects to make them art works, were particularly influential. The works of Manzoni and Klein, Dada, Assemblage, Environments, Happenings and the Fluxus movement were also important, not on the theoretical side, but in making a climate in which personal and apparently arbitrary approaches to art might be considered seriously.

The most pure forms of conceptual art have involved the making of statements which could be direct equivalents or models for objects or the processes of making them. Sol LeWitt wrote in his *Sentences on Conceptual Art* (1968): 'Ideas alone can be works of art; they are in a chain of development that may eventually find some form. All ideas used need not be physical' and 'successful art changes our understanding of the conventions by altering our perceptions'. Joseph Kosuth's works, such as 'Clock (one and five), English/Latin version', 1965, which includes a working clock, a photograph of the clock, and entries from an English/Latin dictionary for 'time', 'machination' and 'object', see art and its context as another 'language' which may be exposed by being 'translated'. This general view of art as a language, or system of signs, reflects the important developments in a structural approach to linguistics and philosophy. Kosuth was for some years associated with the Anglo-American group of conceptual artists, known as Art and Language. The work and publications of this group have contributed to the investigation of art's connections with philosophy and linguistics, while at the same time using parts of the investigation to make art works. Another approach which has concentrated on logic and language is that of Victor Burgin. He has used plain texts, and the juxtaposition of texts with photographs to explore how our reading of images is affected by their context, and the manner in which our understanding of the signs which make up art are conditioned by our culture. John Latham has proposed a whole new philosophy by which an alteration in our understanding of time could affect our understanding of value. This view of the world has been expressed through art works which are partial experiments in these changes. Latham, who was associated with Gustav Metzger's Destruction-in-Art-Symposium in 1966, has, like many of the artists mentioned above, moved from a criticism of culture to a more overtly political criticism of society.

The map has been frequently used by artists because it is a conceptual model with which people are familiar. Works by Douglas Huebler and Dennis Oppenheim have involved the movement of materials from one site to another in the making of 'sculpture' which is not perceived directly, but conceived through maps, photographs and explanatory text. Huebler's works have involved space and extent (through the marking of points bounding shapes across several miles of land), and time (in making 'Duration Pieces' which chart movement or change over a period of time) and ownership (in making works which, for example, have a series of photographs of the owner of the work over ten years). Works such as these chart ecological and human systems and in drawing material from contemporary life, provide a basis for comment and criticism. The late 1960s was a period of general concern for ecology and the conservation of resources which has underpinned much art of the 1970s.

Richard Long has also used maps to plan and record his walks across the landscape which can be considered as sculpture themselves, while also making sculptures

Richard Long, **119 Stones** 1976

(piles of stones, lines of twigs, arrangements of wood) from natural materials along the way and bringing these same materials to be arranged in archetypal shapes in a gallery. The limestone for '119 Stones' came from a quarry near Bristol, and is laid out in a random sequence of stones but in a precisely defined shape. Works by Long, and by Hamish Fulton, focus both on the lyrical, romantic and historic aspects of landscape, and on man's relation to 'nature' around him. Their work (and that of Barry Flanagan, Bruce McLean and Gilbert and George) emerged while they were students on the postgraduate sculpture course run by Frank Martin and Anthony Caro at St Martin's School of Art. David Tremlett has also made 'descriptions' of the landscape while travelling, using drawings, slides and tape recordings to evoke what appears subjectively to be characteristic.

A more 'objective' approach is used by Bernhard and Hilla Becher, who for many years have made art works based on photographs of industrial structures like 'Coal Bunkers'. They make a systematic comparison of the visual relationships between these so-called 'anonymous sculptures', but share with Long, Fulton and Tremlett a strong sense of location and situation. However, the imposition of a tight structure and the composition of works

in series and in serial form is a common characteristic of much art of the 1970s and is visible in otherwise diverse works by Klaus Rinke, Keith Arnatt, Michael Craig-Martin and John Hilliard. The latter three, and the Dutchman Jan Dibbets all make works which challenge our ordinary perception, while exposing the structure and method of their work, as well as projecting an attractive wit and humour. Two people filming each other with hand-held cameras, as they spiral counter-directionally, is the basis of a similar investigation by Dan Graham.

Gilbert and George, the living sculptors, became famous through their singing sculpture 'Underneath the Arches' in which the two artists, their faces and hands painted with metallic paint, slowly circled to the strains of the popular pre-war song. Their works use themselves as a focus for their view of the world, sometimes romantic and lyrical, often poignantly melancholy. Joseph Beuys has also generated a considerable degree of personal myth. He was associated with the Fluxus movement in the late 1950s and through his performances, teaching and political action became an influential and controversial figure in both the worlds of art and politics. His use of Celtic traditions and natural materials, combined with an arcane and poetic vision, is part of the European

Bernhard and Hilla Becher, **Coal Bunkers** 1974

Marcel Broodthaers, **Casserole and Closed Mussels** 1964

culture that emphasises both the personal and the absurd. Marcel Broodthaers was very much part of this culture, though with a particularly strong Belgian streak of the surreal. The 'Casserole and Closed Mussels' uses a Belgian motif (mussels are eaten there like 'fish and chips') and transforms it into an object of grace and wit, the mussels seemingly pushing themselves up into the air, protesting perhaps at their immolation. Ian Hamilton Finlay, like Broodthaers, is both a poet and an artist, combining the lyrical and the humorous in sharply witty works which have extended his original concerns as a 'concrete' poet. 'Lyre (Mk.2)' is a stone relief where a stylised portrayal of a gun set in an oval refers to Cubism, in which musical instruments or domestic objects such as pipes were often used as subject matter. In Finlay's ironic imagery the pipe is seen as a weapon of war.

The Print Collection

Andy Warhol, **Marilyn** 1967 (screenprint)

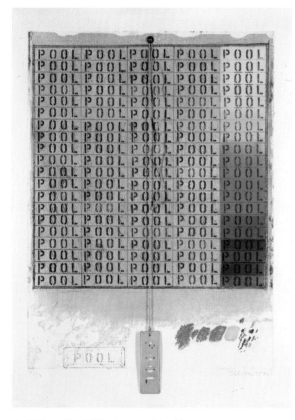

Joe Tilson, **Pool Mantra** 1976 (etching)

This collection was inaugurated in 1975 by the Institute of Contemporary Prints, an organisation that had been formed earlier with the specific intention of beginning a new public collection of contemporary prints within the Tate's Modern Collection. The ICP succeeded in obtaining a great number of gifts from artists, publishers and printers, and handed their entire holding over to the Tate. Under their auspices a central group of major continuing gifts was set up, most notably those from Rose and Chris Prater of Kelpra Studio, Waddington Graphics and the Curwen Studio. The collection continues to expand through the commitment of these and many other generous donors.

The major gifts have shaped the collection and made its greatest strength in the field of British artists' prints from the late sixties to the present. The collection includes a comprehensive collection of Henry Moore's prints to date and considerable groups of work by such artists as Patrick Caulfield, R.B. Kitaj, Eduardo Paolozzi, Richard Smith and Joe Tilson. Some foreign prints are included in the collection, most of them obtained by purchase, including portfolios by Barnett Newman, Sol LeWitt and Andy Warhol, and works by Marcel Broodthaers, Jan Dibbets, Naum Gabo, Jasper Johns and Klaus Rinke. These include certain photographic works which, because they are produced by a printing process, are treated as part of the Print Collection. Although the collection is predominantly contemporary there are some earlier twentieth-century works, including El Lissitzky's *Victory Over the Sun* portfolio published in Hanover in 1923, and the *School Prints* portfolio of 1946, which represents a pioneering attempt to spread the influence of contemporary artists' work as broadly as possible in Britain through specially commissioned prints. A wide range of the media used by artists are represented in the collection, from those traditionally associated with printing craftsmanship like etching to the use of new commercial printing technology in screenprinting or offset photo-lithography.

The primary aim of the collection is to provide examples of work by artists for whom printmaking is particularly important, whose prints should be considered in the context of other works in the Modern Collection. There are also many cases where artists' prints and paintings, sculpture, or other works on paper are closely

interrelated and need to be seen together for a better appreciation of their work. Printmaking allows an artist to make his work available more widely and more cheaply than anything else, but very few artists do it for that reason alone. It is generally done as an extension of other work, and sometimes as a diversion from it. Frequently the discipline of printing methods and co-operation with a master printer and his technicians becomes a stimulus. Some artists have their own presses and are closely concerned with all the processes of printmaking, while others work with master printers in a printing studio. Chris Prater's Kelpra Studio exemplifies the way a studio should put the full range of techniques and skills at an artist's disposal, while being flexible enough to respond to his particular working methods. Although some artists print and publish their own editions, a vital contribution is made by publishers who enable artists to make prints by commissioning and underwriting the edition.

El Lissitzky, **Victory over the Sun: 1. Part of the Spectacle Machinery** 1923 (lithograph)

R.B. Kitaj, **French Subjects** 1974 (screenprint)

[152]